ONE ON ONE

AA Sponsorship in Action

BOOKS PUBLISHED BY AA GRAPEVINE, INC.

The Language of the Heart (& eBook)
The Best of the Grapevine Volume I (eBook only)
The Best of Bill (& eBook)
Thank You for Sharing
Spiritual Awakenings (& eBook)
I Am Responsible: The Hand of AA
The Home Group: Heartbeat of AA (& eBook)
Emotional Sobriety — The Next Frontier (& eBook)
Spiritual Awakenings II (& eBook)
In Our Own Words: Stories of Young AAs in Recovery (& eBook)
Beginners' Book (& eBook)
Voices of Long-Term Sobriety (& eBook)
A Rabbit Walks Into A Bar
Step by Step — Real AAs, Real Recovery (& eBook)
Emotional Sobriety II — The Next Frontier (& eBook)
Young & Sober (& eBook)
Into Action (& eBook)
Happy, Joyous & Free (& eBook)
One on One (& eBook)
No Matter What (& eBook)
Grapevine Daily Quote Book (& eBook)
Sober & Out (& eBook)
Forming True Partnerships (& eBook)
Our Twelve Traditions (& eBook)
Making Amends (& eBook)
Voices of Women in AA (& eBook)
AA in the Military (& eBook)
One Big Tent (& eBook)

IN SPANISH

El lenguaje del corazón
Lo mejor de Bill (& eBook)
El grupo base: Corazón de AA
Lo mejor de La Viña
Felices, alegres y libres (& eBook)
Un día a la vez (& eBook)
Frente A Frente (& eBook)

IN FRENCH

Le langage du coeur
Les meilleurs articles de Bill
Le Groupe d'attache: Le battement du coeur des AA
En tête à tête (& eBook)
Heureux, joyeux et libres (& eBook)

ONE ON ONE

AA Sponsorship in Action

AA GRAPEVINE, Inc.
New York, New York
WWW.AAGRAPEVINE.ORG

475 Riverside Drive
New York, New York 10115

ISBN: 978-1-938413-18-6

Printed in Canada

Third Printing 2019

AA PREAMBLE

Alcoholics Anonymous is a fellowship of men and women
who share their experience, strength and hope
with each other that they may solve their common problem
and help others to recover from alcoholism.

The only requirement for membership is a desire to stop drinking.
There are no dues or fees for AA membership; we are self-
supporting through our own contributions. AA is not allied with
any sect, denomination, politics, organization or institution;
does not wish to engage in any controversy, neither endorses nor
opposes any causes.

Our primary purpose is to stay sober and help other alcoholics
to achieve sobriety.

CONTENTS

CHAPTER EIGHT

NOTHING IN COMMON?

Old/young, gay/straight—unlikely pairs bond as sponsor and sponsee

CHAPTER NINE

START EACH DAY WITH A MIRACLE

These desperate alcoholics never thought AA would work for them. But working with their sponsors, they broke through and started to recover

CHAPTER TEN

GROUP HUG

When sponsorship becomes a team effort

WELCOME

It was at Bill W.'s kitchen table that he and Ebby T. formed the first sponsee/sponsor relationship. "He had come to pass his experience along to me—if I cared to have it," Bill wrote in his story, the first chapter in the Big Book. "Certainly I was interested. I had to be, for I was hopeless."

Ebby T., a former schoolmate and occasional drinking buddy, had gotten sober through the Oxford Group and had been told to carry the message of hope to others. But Ebby's message to Bill wasn't just sympathy for a suffering man. He told Bill that if he wanted to get better, he had to change. Ebby started working with him on making amends and getting rid of character defects. "I fully acquainted him with my problems and deficiencies," Bill continues, describing in the Big Book the early work he did with Ebby: "We made a list of people I had hurt or toward whom I felt resentment. I expressed my entire willingness to approach these individuals, admitting my wrong. ... My friend had emphasized the absolute necessity of demonstrating these principles in all my affairs. Particularly was it imperative to work with others as he had worked with me." That message led to Bill finding Dr. Bob, and they became sponsor/sponsee. As the AA program grew and its founders began to work with others, the flame of sponsorship was passed along—and it continues to burn today.

"In AA, sponsor and sponsored meet as equals, just as Bill and Dr. Bob did," says the AA pamphlet, *Questions & Answers on Sponsorship*. "Essentially, the process of sponsorship is this: An alcoholic who has made some progress in the recovery program shares that experience on a continuous, individual basis with another alcoholic who is attempting to attain or maintain sobriety through AA."

In this book, members write about the joys and challenges of sponsorship, the many ways we do it, and how we consider it a vital key to staying sober as well as living a happy life. "Alcoholics recovered in AA want to share what they have learned with other alcoholics," *Questions & Answers on Sponsorship* says. "We know from experience that our own sobriety is greatly strengthened when we give it away!" There is no right or wrong way to sponsor, only suggestions—each sponsor and sponsee finds his or her own path.

CHAPTER ONE

I WOULD NOT STAND A CHANCE ALONE

AA members talk about how they define sponsorship

"Sponsorship is a bridge to trusting the human race, the very race we once resigned from. In learning to trust, we are strengthening our sobriety," writes the author of "A Means to a Beginning." "A sponsor's only job (and only area of expertise) is to help fellow alcoholics not take that first drink by passing this program on to others as it was passed on to him or her in order to stay sober," adds the author of "Shopping For a Sponsor. "The only qualification is his or her own experience learning to stay and live sober." In the stories that follow, AAs talk about how they see and experience sponsorship.

Have You a Sponsor?

January 1975

What can be done for the alcoholic who is a newcomer in AA, who has suffered one traumatic experience after another, one failure after another, who is desperately willing to reconstruct his life, yet unable to do it himself? How can hope be instilled in him, to replace despair? How can a recovering alcoholic find calm and something that was never in him before—patience? How can a person who has repeatedly failed all his life be convinced that things will get better, especially when he will not even be in control of his own life?

Like everything else in AA, the answer is simple. The key to success for the alcoholic, to repairs for an emotionally mangled life, lies in AA sponsorship. Sponsorship by its very nature demands complete honesty and gut-level communication between the sponsor and the newcomer.

I speak from my own observations, but mostly from my own experience. I do believe God's will is being projected through my sponsor. I thank God that my sponsor has intervened in my life when I started straying, especially when I was doing something that could interfere with someone else's way of life. At many of these interventions, I objected vehemently, but I later accepted the fact that I was sick.

I would not stand a chance alone. In the past, I did everything recommended by AA except getting a sponsor, and for a long time I stayed frustrated and baffled, wondering what had gone wrong.

When I drank, I had a drinking problem that I could not handle. When I stopped drinking, I had a living problem that I could not cope with—I had no idea even where to begin. But

I am stepping along now, and those steps feel a lot more secure with the help of my sponsor.

L. W.
Syracuse, New York

A Means to a Beginning (Excerpt)

February 1984

I picked out a sponsor who had reasonable sobriety, seven years, and was walking the walk. He told me, "Come follow me. I'll show you how to ..." I learned that sponsors are people with open minds, who suggest things to their "sponsees" or "pigeons." They show us by example. They are not a means to an end, but a means to a beginning. They teach us how to participate in our own recovery by participating in life. They are a bridge to other members. Sponsors show us a picture of the whole of AA, beyond the meetings. They teach us about the Three Legacies. Sure, the first is Recovery—the Twelve Steps; but we must also keep this thing together—Unity, the Twelve Traditions; and we must carry the message—the Third Legacy, Service, guided by the Twelve Concepts.

The AA pamphlet "Questions and Answers on Sponsorship" states, "Experience shows clearly that the members getting the most out of the AA program, and the groups doing the best job of carrying the AA message to still-suffering alcoholics, are those for whom sponsorship is too important to be left to chance."

Sponsorship is a bridge to trusting the human race, the very race we once resigned from. In learning to trust, we are strengthening our sobriety. And the benefit goes two ways. The Big Book best explains this: "Practical experience shows that nothing will so much insure immunity from drinking as intensive work with other alcoholics." Or, to quote a friend and longtime AA member: "A man is no fool to give away something he cannot keep in order to get something he cannot lose."

M. S.
Grand Island, Nebraska

Shopping For a Sponsor

May 2003

It took many years (and many relapses) before I understood the value of sponsorship. I had to learn the hard way that the word "I" does not exist in the Twelve Steps of Alcoholics Anonymous. I was my own sponsor for many years, and I got the results one might expect: repeated relapses, much frustration, and a deep sense of failure. I did not find the happiness, sense of purpose, and joy I heard about from others in Alcoholics Anonymous until I surrendered, and we (my sponsors and I) started to walk this journey together.

Newcomers frequently ask me how to choose a sponsor. Looking back, I now see that I've probably spent more time choosing a dress or CD than I've spent choosing the person who would help me with the most important task in my life—living sober, one day at a time.

Today, I am blessed with two wonderful sponsors, both solid AAs, and each a gift from God, who came when I became willing to become teachable. From their examples, this is what I have learned about what sponsors are and are not.

What sponsors are not:

Sponsors are not guidance counselors, marital counselors, lawyers, nor doctors. (I have seen tragic results from well-intentioned sponsors advising their sponsees to discontinue medications without their regular doctors' consent.)

Sponsors are not bankers, mortgage companies, nor other financial institutions.

Sponsors are not babysitters, best friends, nor preachers.

Sponsors are not dictators or drill sergeants.

Sponsors are not God.

Then what, you may be wondering, do sponsors do?

When I asked my sponsor this question, she suggested that I

read the seventh chapter of the Big Book, "Working with Others." A sponsor's only job (and only area of expertise) is to help fellow alcoholics not take that first drink by passing this program on to others as it was passed on to him or her in order to stay sober. The only qualification is his or her own experience learning to stay and live sober, and the gift a sponsor gives is the hope, should another alcoholic care to listen, that he or she might do the same.

With this in mind, here are some other questions I learned to consider when choosing a sponsor:

Does he or she truly walk the walk, or simply talk the talk? (I learn best from demonstrations, not lectures.)

Is she or he active in service work?

Do they speak from their own experience?

Does he or she refer to the Big Book, the "Twelve and Twelve," and other AA literature when they speak?

Most importantly, is she or he happy in sobriety? I spent years in the miserable darkness of alcoholism. I did not know what real happiness was when I came through the doors of AA. I needed someone to teach me, by example, how to live in peace and joy and service in this world through the Steps and fellowship of this program. I believe that happiness and joy are a result of taking the Steps and doing the next right thing. I cannot do this or any part of the program alone and today, thanks to the God of my understanding, the program of Alcoholics Anonymous, and my sponsors, I never have to again.

RITA H.
Greensboro, North Carolina

The Silent Sponsor (Excerpt)

December 1964

I have heard certain members of AA say that they were able to make the program without feeling the need for a sponsor. Others contend that they have never played the part of a sponsor, although they admit to being active in other ways. These are honest statements and represent a large number of AAs, perhaps even a majority, who have been able to find sobriety either without knowingly picking a sponsor or being picked, or both. However, I believe that sponsorship may also be an unspoken phenomenon—a natural result of the newcomer's need for guidance and the older member's sense of responsibility toward the newcomer.

A newcomer will almost always encounter at least one older member whom he likes, looks up to or respects. He will listen to him, discuss problems with him and even try to emulate him. At these moments sponsorship is taking place without the word sponsor ever having been mentioned. In many cases the new member may not even be aware of what the word means, if in fact he has heard it at all, until he has reached the point in his recovery where he no longer really needs a sponsor in the academic sense.

I believe that we should never insist on a formalized sponsorship. If a newcomer learns to rely too heavily on any one member he may become too one-sided in his thinking, or he may become overly dependent on his sponsor. As I see it, proper guidance in AA must come from a group rather than an individual; the newcomer is cheating himself if he allows any one member to dominate his thinking. A newcomer should learn to stand on his own feet and eventually take his place in the group, independent of any outside influence except the Higher Power.

J. S. C.
New Hartford, New York

A Canadian Sponsor's Program (Excerpt)

February 1953

In my belief the most important responsibility the sponsor has to the new member, is example.

There is no use running around like a hen on a hot griddle while preaching "easy does it."

No use allowing bigotry to ooze from one's every utterance while talking about an open mind.

No use boasting about one's great plans for the future years while attempting to show the virtue of the twenty-four-hour program.

No use for the sponsor to describe the beauties of contented sobriety to the newcomer while he, the sponsor, is on a "dry drunk."

Example is man's most powerful force for good or evil. To me, the debts hardest to repay are to those I harmed by bad example, and thus do I believe that my greatest responsibility to those whom God has given me the grace to sponsor, and to AA as a whole, is the good example I can give by practicing the principles of the Twelve Steps in all my affairs.

G. K.
Kirkland Lake, Ontario

A Sponsor Is ... (Excerpt)

August 1985

The kind of question I like to hear from a newcomer is "What's a sponsor?" It shows he's been listening, and I am happy to respond. Secretly, I hope he thinks he already knows the answer and is introducing the subject in order to find out if I am willing to become his sponsor.

My own sponsor has a good way of putting things. His definition: “A person whose opinions you have learned to trust; someone whose advice you know you are going to follow before you get there to state the problem.”

It was a twelfth-stepper, rather than a sponsor, who first brought me to AA, from a psycho unit. I didn’t consider myself “one of those alcoholics.” Even if I was, I was certainly too intelligent to need a sponsor. Besides, I had no intention of continuing with AA; I was only checking it out to keep my psychiatrist happy. I had discovered that happiness on a psycho unit is having a happy psychiatrist.

I didn’t ask anyone to be my sponsor until the men’s stag group got after me for thinking myself too highbrow to need one. Since then, I have had absolutely fabulous experiences both in having a sponsor and in being a sponsor to others. I’m not sure which has been of greater value and have no intention of giving up either.

Who should have a sponsor? Our group thinks everyone should. Since we are all equal, how could it be otherwise? Obviously, persons new to the program need more frequent contact with their sponsors than those with years of happy sobriety, but we all need a confidant.

Since the Big Book doesn’t have a chapter on sponsorship etiquette, we just pick up ideas as we go along. The most important considerations about a sponsor are: to have one, to use one, and when asked, to agree to be one.

There isn’t any single “right” answer to the question “What’s a sponsor?” But an entirely appropriate answer to the question “Will you be my sponsor?” is “Sure! Let’s have some coffee and talk about it.”

P.O.
Claremont, California

Sponsorship (Excerpt)

February 1955

All of us are acquainted with individuals who measure their success in AA by the number of people they have sponsored who "make" the program. Some consider it a failure on their part when someone they have contacted or sponsored fails to remain sober. As far as my own success or failure on this program is concerned, it makes little difference whether my "baby" makes the program or not. Naturally I like to see him make it for his own good, but the important thing, for me, is that I have tried. I have tried to "carry the message" and tried to give what has been given to me.

It is very possible that I might not be the most suitable person to sponsor a particular new member. I might be unsuited by my personality, by my education (or lack of education) or by my profession. For the same reasons I might be just the one to sponsor someone else. It is my belief that the more we have in common with a prospective member the more help we can be as a sponsor.

Because of the very nature of an alcoholic, the approach used to convince one individual that AA is the solution to his problem will not necessarily work for another prospect. Many members use the same approach on all prospective new members whom they contact, when actually we should pattern our methods to suit the personality of the individual with whom we are working.

R. L. O.
Lawton, Oklahoma

Closed Meeting

July 1961

"If you travel in a foreign land," said one of our older members, "you need a map and a guide. For us, in the new land of sober living, the program is our map and a sponsor is our guide. Our sponsor can help us to understand and to work the program, and is the desirable person with whom to do the Fifth Step when we are ready for it."

ANONYMOUS
New York City, New York

My Sponsor, My Friend

August 1982

When I came into AA, I was told to get a sponsor. The word itself confused me, but I began looking. At a meeting one night, I heard a girl talking. She sounded so nice and her story sounded so much like mine that right away I asked her to be my sponsor.

As time went by, we became very close friends, but I did not feel that she was helping me. I really loved her as a friend, but she always seemed to want to control me and my life, when I only wanted advice. Whenever we were together and she asked what Step I was on or brought up anything that had to do with AA, I changed the subject. I guess you could say I ran. This went on for many months, and I kept thinking, Well, I have to get a different sponsor.

One night, I was going to tell her that I would have to let her go. You know what the outcome of our talk was? We became closer than we had ever been, as sponsor and sponsee. I found out why I had felt she was not the right sponsor for me. It was not her so much as it was me.

I had built a wall between us that I could not break through. I realized we had seemed to be growing away from each other because I was not letting her see me. How am I supposed to get help from any sponsor if I do not let her see who I am and where I am at? I was afraid that if I let her see me, I would be judged, and I didn't want that—I wanted everyone to believe I was well. I wanted to be where everyone else in the program was, rather where I was. That night, I opened up and let her know that I was not where I pretended to be.

I am sick, but I am getting better slowly. I now feel that I can talk to my sponsor, not from my mouth, but from my heart. It does hurt to let people know that you're not as well as you want to be, but I want to get better. Running from where I am is not going to get me better. So I am working today with the help of my sponsor.

S. D.
Chicago, Illinois

More Questions Than Answers

March 1989

Last night at one of my favorite meetings, a friend pulled me aside to ask for some help with a newcomer she was sponsoring. She needed to talk, and I needed to hear myself say, "What do you or I or anyone know about sponsorship anyway?" even though I have spent hours, days, months, and years working with newcomers in the Fellowship.

Sponsorship and service are without a doubt the foundation of my sobriety and my happiness. In service work I am profoundly aware that the more I learn the more there is to learn. But until a few months ago, I thought I had a lot of good ideas—certainly a lot of opinions—about sponsorship. After all, I spend a couple of hours every day being a sponsor to various women, and since some success had attended these efforts, I felt I knew something. In my better moments, I saw working with newcomers as simply the work I did for the God of my understanding on a daily basis. Since I had never yet asked, "Will you be my pigeon?" I assumed the people put in my life were the ones God meant me to work with, to help as best I could, with the tremendous support of the Fellowship. Since I turned my pigeons over to him on a daily basis, I simply tried to serve in any way possible, whether on the phone, at a meeting, for lunch or for coffee. The single most important thing I did as a sponsor was to show up and then let go and let God.

But I felt that some relationships were smoother—better, easier, more gratifying for me. Consequently, I assumed that these better relationships were the ones in which I most successfully did God's work. If I ever had to get rid of a few pigeons, these easy relationships would be the ones that I would keep. Because the others, on occasion, drove me wild.

That was a few months ago. Then, as the "Twelve and Twelve" says, life has a way of handing us a few lumps. Returning from my honeymoon, I received a call that one of my most beloved pigeons had committed suicide. I cannot even write these words without crying; at many moments the pain and the loss are still greater than the acceptance. I have asked myself repeatedly: "Why? Why didn't I give her my out-of-town phone number? Why didn't I have one more conversation with her?" My last vision of her is at the wedding, happy, laughing, and smiling. Sponsoring her had been pure joy; there was never a harsh word between us. She ended every conversation by telling me she loved me; I never doubted that she did. She was one of the easiest people to love unconditionally I have ever known.

You don't take credit for your successes and you don't take credit for your failures, old-time wisdom tells us. I believe that, and yet I felt that I had failed her, failed the Fellowship, and failed the God of my understanding. But how limited is my own wisdom?

Yesterday, another one of my pigeons was on the phone. I had just given her a three-year medallion the night before. She casually said, "You know, I think we have had the perfect sponsor and pigeon relationship." From my point of view the statement was shocking. We had argued frequently, she had rebelled against all the suggestions of the program, had refused to go to meetings, and in my opinion had been on a dry drunk for months at a time. It was certainly true that in the past few months she was beginning to work at the Steps and was starting to take some responsibility for her actions and her sobriety. Maybe it *was* the ideal relationship because she and I are still sober and because I didn't quit, as I often wanted to do, and tell God this was work I wouldn't do. All I could do, it seemed to me, was to hang in a day at a time.

I am at one of those points where there are more questions than answers. I still believe that when I watch the newcomers I sponsor get active, go to meetings, work with a group, reach out to others in the Fellowship, attend Step meetings, and begin to get their foundation in the program, I am more or less doing what I am supposed to do as a sponsor. I also know that there are moments when a pigeon calls to tell me she is a sponsor for the first time—when she becomes my peer in the Fellowship, doing the work of AA—that make me happy. When a pigeon stands at the podium and talks about how glad she was to get her first year so that she could give service to the Fellowship I feel I am on the right path. But those are things I value. What does God want?

No doubt I have complicated sponsorship. Whatever happens to those I sponsor, working with them has kept me sober and for that I am profoundly grateful. I know that as long as God keeps putting people in my life, I will keep on being a sponsor. Whether that is for a day or for years is simply God's will and not mine. Like all my gifts in this life, these pigeons are simply on loan from God and can be called back by him, or to him, at any time.

A. S.
Dorchester, Massachusetts

CHAPTER TWO

DISCIPLINE SAVED MY LIFE

How following a sponsor's directions led to recovery and growth

In the story "Beyond 'I'm Sorry'," when one sponsor suggests to an AA that he make amends to a client he'd harmed in the past by offering his services free of charge, his sponsee responds, "Uhhh ... I'll have to think about that." But when the sponsee does follow his sponsor's suggestion, he gets positive results and knows it was what he needed to do. In "My Good Sponsor," a struggling newbie laughs when his sponsor suggests he make coffee. "A year or two later, after more experimenting and more benders, I made the coffee! I did not know it then, but I was on my way," the author writes.

The stories in this chapter are about sponsees following direction from their sponsors—some willingly, some not so willingly—and seeing the results.

Disciplinary Measures

November 2010

One of the most important things I have learned from my sponsors is discipline. Without it, I would slowly but surely revert back to my old ways or suddenly find myself caught up in that critical unguarded moment we sometimes speak of.

I don't believe that the program is hard to do, despite the fact that I didn't believe it would work for me, and at first I had no love of Step work. My program doesn't require that much "work" these days, but it does require persistent action on my part.

On my first day in AA I asked for a sponsor and he told me that I needed to do five things every day. I wrote them down inside the front cover of my newly purchased Big Book and continue this custom with the men I sponsor.

I have heard slight variations on these things in the years that I've been in the Fellowship. As he related them to me, they were:

Don't drink.

Pray at least twice a day. (In the morning ask God to take away my desire to drink, and in the evening thank him for keeping me sober.)

Go to an AA meeting.

Read some AA literature.

Talk to another alcoholic.

None of my sponsors (I've had three in my nine years) has ever suggested that I discontinue any of these practices. I continue them to this day with only minor deviation. I say the Third Step Prayer in the mornings and sometimes only go to five or six meetings a week.

Do I really need that many meetings at this point in my sobriety? Only God knows for sure. Anyway, I like to go most of the time to see if I can be helpful to someone else. This question leads me to the story that I wanted to relate.

In 1982 I was a soldier in the U.S. Cavalry doing field training in the Yakima desert. I worked flight operations for the Army. My "office" when in the field was a M588 armored personnel carrier and I was about half asleep at two or three in the morning one night while pulling radio watch. There was no radio chatter, and I was bored out of my mind when I saw that the generators needed to be fueled. I went to the back of the vehicle and grabbed a five gallon can of gas and headed for the commander's hatch.

As I was passing my work station I grabbed my helmet off my desk without thinking about it and put it on. I had been trained to do this anytime I went outside while in the field. I continued to the commander's hatch and began climbing the short ladder that would take me outside (climbing with one hand and holding the can in the other). I reached the hatch and got a rather precarious grip on the ladder with the hand that was holding the gas can. I took one more step up the ladder as I threw the hatch back with one arm.

Hatches on armored personnel carriers are approximately three feet in diameter, made of solid steel and spring-loaded. When I threw the hatch upward I didn't use quite enough force. Looking back, I can clearly remember hearing the hatch touch the latch mechanism, but I did not hear the latch engage.

The next thing I knew, I was on my butt at the bottom of the ladder with a terrific headache. That massive piece of steel had hit me squarely on top of the head with tremendous force. Had it not been for my "steel pot," I would have surely suffered a crushed skull and died there on the spot.

What motivated me to grab that helmet at the one crucial moment that would unwittingly be a matter of life and death? I, along with most soldiers, had great disdain for wearing those steel pots. They weighed about eight pounds, were uncomfortable, and generally speaking were a pain in the rear, so I didn't really want to put it on. We were not in real combat and no one would be shooting at me, so I didn't think I needed to have it on. It was the middle of the night and no one was around. All the sergeants and officers were asleep, so no one would yell at me for not wearing it.

I put it on without thinking, simply because that is what I was trained (or disciplined) to do. On this occasion at least, that discipline saved my life.

Discipline can be defined as doing what is necessary, regardless of whether you want to or whether you think you need to. Discipline has a brother named courage, which could be defined as applying discipline in the face of fear (but that's another story).

What does this have to do with being sober? There are times I don't want to go to meetings or do those five things every day. There are times when I would rather be sleeping in my warm comfy bed than talking to someone who's having trouble, or getting up at seven on Sundays to have breakfast with my AA family. There are certainly times when I don't feel like I need to do those five things.

The thing is, I don't know which meeting or on what occasion doing one of those five things will literally save my life. I would hate to miss the one I really needed for lack of discipline.

JOHNNY L.
Madison, Tennessee

What Sober Women Wear to Bed

June 1988

I spent my first day without a drink or a drug frantically reading the Big Book, trying to learn if I had the disease of alcoholism. I had begged my husband to tell me, but he insisted it was something I had to figure out for myself. So he handed me the hefty blue volume, told me I'd find my answer in there, and left for work.

I read all day and went to my first meeting that night.

My mouth was dry on the second day, but I didn't drink and went to a meeting.

The itching started on the third day, so I scratched and went to a meeting—and got a sponsor.

On the fourth day I continued to scratch, went to a meeting, and called my sponsor. That night, my husband held me until I fell asleep.

By the fifth day everything tasted like metal and I thought I'd go nuts. So I called my sponsor and went to a meeting. Afterward, my husband held me some more.

I came apart the sixth day, sobbed uncontrollably through two meetings and, at the suggestion of my sponsor, agreed to go to a rehab.

Much of that evening remains blurred, but I do remember taking my toothbrush out of the bathroom cabinet and putting it in my purse. Then I went to the bedroom and took a stained and misshapen red T-shirt out of a drawer.

"And what is that?" my sponsor asked.

"What the *@Â§Â©#â€ â€¡*! do you mean?" I answered in fear, pain, and anger. "That's my nightgown."

"Sober women don't wear things like that to bed," Jean said. I was in no shape to argue. The T-shirt stayed home.

When I asked what I should take to sleep in, Jean told me not to worry about it. So I didn't.

That night I slept in my underwear and a hospital gown. I awoke in the morning cloaked in the pain, fear, and anger of the night before. A patient asked a question and I replied with vulgarities.

"Sober women don't talk like that," she said.

"*Â©â€¡#â€ *!" I told her. And then I thought about what she had just taught me—and about what my sponsor had taught me the night before.

Both messages had to do with how sober women behaved—or didn't behave, in my case. And that's how I began learning how a sober woman acts, talks, thinks, and dresses. Luckily, I haven't had to figure that out on my own, for hundreds of sober women attend the nightly meetings I attend. Their example has taught me.

During the past fourteen months of my recovery, I've learned a lot about living life as a sober woman.

Oh, about what sober women wear to bed: My sponsor brought me a gaily wrapped gift my first day in rehab. Inside it were a silky blue nightgown and a matching robe. That, I learned, is what sober women wear to bed.

Months later I realized I had learned something even more important: the lengths a sponsor will go to to show a woman how to get sober and to pass on the love of the sisterhood available in Alcoholics Anonymous.

DODIE W.
Plainsboro, New Jersey

Beyond "I'm Sorry"

September 2009

I was just out of rehab and getting involved in AA in my community. I got a sponsor, and I told him about the mess I'd left behind on my last drunken spree. I work as a freelance graphic designer and was in the middle of several projects for an ad agency. It was St. Patrick's Day and I'd decided to tie one on because, after all, I'm Irish-American.

My drinking spree went beyond the holiday and continued for another four or five days. I avoided my wife, daughter, home and work. I went from bar to bar until my ATM card wouldn't work anymore. After I came home I lay in bed, very sick. I kept hearing calls on the answering machine from my client, pleading with me to get ahold of him. I didn't. I did have enough sense to throw myself into rehab with the help and support of my wonderful wife.

I told my sponsor about the jam I'd left my client in by avoiding his calls and the pending projects that I was working on. He suggested that I make amends to the client. I said, "What, walk into his office and apologize? I don't know if I can do that."

My sponsor said, "No, you'll do more than that. You'll walk into his office, apologize, then you'll offer your services at no charge until you make up for the damage you created."

I said, "Uhhh ... I'll have to think about that."

A couple of weeks or so later, the thought of that amends popped into my head as I was driving home at about 10 in the morning. It became increasingly obvious to me that this was the right time to walk into that office and do what I needed to do. Yikes!

I was scared to death. What if he gets angry with me? What if he throws me out of his office? What if ... Then I thought of something that might help: praying. I live in a mountain community, and as I was driving up the highway I saw beautiful views below the cliffs. I pulled off the road into a turnout, got out of the car and got down on my knees. I asked my Higher Power to help me and to remove my fear. I asked him for his will, not mine, and to speak his words through my mouth as I made this amends. I finished praying, stood up and turned around. There was a vast, beautiful view as I gazed down the mountainside. I felt very much at peace. I really don't know if I had a spiritual awakening that morning, but it certainly felt like something of that nature.

I got back in the car and drove to my client's office, a little more comfortable now. I walked up to the front desk and the receptionist said, "Hi, Rick," as if she had just seen me the day before. I took a seat and had to wait before I entered the bigwig's office. He came out and said, "Hi, Rick. Come on in." I sat down in his office, quickly asked my Higher Power to be with me once again, took a deep breath and began.

I told him that I have a problem with alcohol, that I'd just come out of rehab and that I'm in recovery. I told him that I was fully aware of abandoning my responsibilities to him and the projects, and that I had jeopardized the relationship and reputation between his company and the clients. I told him that I was sorry. He responded with, "I'm so glad that you're taking care of your life. How is your family?" Wow, I thought to myself. He's not as angry as I thought. I then told him that I needed to make up for the mess that I created, and I offered my services at no charge for a couple of work days. He seemed to be caught off guard for a few seconds, then said, "Okay, if you feel that you need to do that." So that's exactly what I did.

I had no ulterior motive when making this amends, nor did I ever expect to work for that agency again. But I have to end this story now, because I need to get back to work on a fairly big project for that very client.

RICK M.
California

Why It Works

October 2010

I must admit that when I first looked over our Twelve Traditions hanging on the wall, I thought they were a dumb, boring business charter. I was so smart that I knew they had nothing to do with me, and with that information, I ignored them for as long as I could. That was until the day my sponsor, wise woman that she was, suggested that I go through the Traditions with her just as we had the Steps. It seemed like a corny idea at the time, but she was my sponsor and I did not know you could tell your sponsor no. (I still don't recommend that.)

One by one we read them together, studying page after page, looking for the spiritual principles and the practical applications.

Though at the time I did not understand the significance they would have in my life or how much wisdom was within the words on the page, I know today that they are "why it works" and they are also, when practiced in my own life, the glue that allows unity in my relationships with others inside and outside the rooms of AA.

My sponsor taught me to take each Tradition and find how it applied to me personally. When I felt stuck and could not see the spiritual significance or application, she encouraged me to dig deeper. She shared her own experience about what the Traditions had brought to her own life. When I struggled with finances and debt, and with my husband wanting to set a budget, she shared with me the freedom I would experience by being self-supporting through my own contributions.

When I wanted to complain about my husband or mother-in-law one more time, she shared with me that having no opinion on outside issues might save me from some resentments.

She said that the common welfare of my family should come first. She said I should stick to my own side of the street and be self-governing, and in this autonomy I would have peace of mind. She said that everyone, including myself, had the right to be wrong.

And she taught me that keeping my mouth shut and not playing the big shot was a great way to practice anonymity, for it is only by staying right-sized with humility that I can practice the spiritual principles I learned before I let my personality run the show.

HEATHER L.
Oceanside, California

My Good Sponsor

July 1973

It was some thirteen years ago, but I can remember every detail as though it happened only a few hours ago. I was in a railroad station, looking out and across the street, waiting for a package-store owner to open up shop. My body was trembling, and my sense of balance was so bad that each step required muscular direction—and I was sober. But I had picked up that first drink after a six-month dry period, and now the most important thing in my life was to get a bottle.

Even from a drunkalog as brief as what I've just written, you should know that I was a guy who did not believe in the "progression" and "first drink" theories. I played at AA for about four years before I surrendered to the facts of AA and accepted my own responsibility to myself. Yes, I realized that I needed to get sober and stay sober and that I had AA to go to—but I wanted AA members to come up with "their" sobriety and present it to me on some kind of painless, effortless platter.

I had admitted and accepted my alcoholism, but I could not advance from there to the all-important part of getting sober—doing something about it!

Many alcoholics I have met in recent years are up on alcoholism. Too few are up on sobriety. When we get finished discussing the disease of alcoholism and its unfortunate victims, we have to take a good "tough love" approach. Few victims of this illness can expect sobriety without a major change in most aspects of living. Family reacceptance, job reliability, and social integration are our goals at the beginning stages of sobriety. They are not easy to achieve, and this is where the Fellowship can support and encourage. Every recovering alcoholic, during the first tries for sobriety, has at some time or other figured himself or herself to be unique. Not one of us is. Each of us has traveled this same rocky road. You are not alone, and if you can put yourself into gear, but stay out of the driver's seat at the same time, you can do it.

I, for one, believe strongly in having a good sponsor. But how do you define a good sponsor? To me, a sponsor's worth can't be measured on some kind of evaluation scale. My good sponsor was a guy who could relate with me and who believed that I would someday make it. In spite of my sick resistance, he guided me toward getting active in the group. He took me on a Twelfth Step call, and I got nothing from it. He suggested that I make coffee for the group meeting, and I laughed.

A year or two later, after more experimenting and more benders, I made the coffee! I did not know it then, but I was on my way. People commented on my skill or lack of skill with the coffee pot. My ego was getting a face-lifting, and my sponsor was watching.

After about a year of continued sobriety, using the sponsor and the group for support, I was asked to chair a meeting. It came at a good time. It seemed as though they were saying, "Joe, we are proud of you, and this is our vote of confidence." Yeah, I know—you could call this pride on my part, and pride can be bad. It wasn't for me! I dove into the responsibility of being secretary, and it was a godsend.

My sponsor stood off to the side then and, I think, secretly beamed. Actually, he was beaming for AA, for without it, we might both be still drinking—or dead.

JOE H.
Rocky Hill, Connecticut

How My Sponsor Got Better

December 1982

At a recent meeting, the topic was the indispensability of sponsors. Member after eloquent member shared experiences with marvelous, mind-reading super-people. I got the impression that sponsors were universally loved; no one seemed to have any complaints.

"Pedestaling" of sponsors scares me, even though I know that my fellow members were sharing experiences and that those eulogies were their perceptions of sponsors. My experience was a little different.

When I first came to these rooms, I met a very formidable woman whom I asked (in fear, trembling, and ignorance) to be my sponsor. She had lots of demands. She knew exactly what she wanted of me. She demanded that I go to meetings. She suggested, with gimlet eye fastened to mine, that I go to ninety meetings in ninety days. She insisted I call her every day. And she expected me to absolutely not drink, one day at a time.

I soon discovered that she didn't understand me—that I had special problems, that I was especially intelligent. She didn't have a sense of humor, either, and I knew she'd have to be replaced.

But I did what she told me to: I went to at least one meeting each day, and each day I didn't drink for one day. I called her every day and talked both her ears off.

I don't know how—but this program works. She got better. She became the most patient, caring person I knew. She became able to interpret the Steps to me, and she became adept at sorting out my feelings—a jumbled mass of nerves wanting a drink. She always made me feel better when I called her, and that skill helped me to get some happily sober days. Best of all, this angel developed a sense of humor.

She and I both stayed sober. And while I don't know how this program works, I do know it worked for her, and of course, she owes it all to me. And of course, you always love someone you have helped, and I do.

A. M.
White Plains, New York

Raving Sober (From Dear Grapevine)

October 2008

I was sober six years—stark raving sober—in a dry drunk with untreated alcoholism, when Jenn H. became my sponsor. She met with me on a regular basis and read the Big Book with me and to me. She explained it to me, and I was finally ready and willing.

She taught me so much and gave me so much of her time that by the time we got to Chapter Five, where the Third Step is located, I was ready. She instructed me to "immediately" start the Fourth Step. She worked through all the Steps with me, Big Book in hand. Through prayer and her guidance, I was reborn.

Since then, I have sponsored exactly the same way. I am listening to my sponsee's Fourth Step this Friday. Thanks to God, AA, and a great sponsor, I now have been sober fourteen years.

KANDY K.
Clarksburg, West Virginia

CHAPTER THREE

THERE ARE NO BOSSES

Finding our own ways to sponsor and be sponsored

While the previous chapter explored the benefits of following direction, especially when new in AA, in this chapter recovering alcoholics take another view—that of individuality in sponsorship; being a guide rather than a rule-maker. Says the author of "Live and Let Live," "There is not a society on earth that places greater emphasis on the individual's right to think, say, and do what he or she pleases than AA."

And in "What a Sponsor Is and Is Not," the author writes, "Today I have a clearer perspective on what my role as a sponsor is and isn't. It is to stay sober, be available to listen, share my thoughts, pray for others, and let them live their own lives. It is not to 'fix' anyone, get them sober, make them happy, demand they conform, or make their decisions." In the pages that follow, AAs talk about following their hearts and not necessarily following or giving direction.

Sponsorship Is a Two-Way Street

September 1988

I was exceptionally skeptical the first time I heard someone say, "Sponsorship helps the sponsor at least as much as it helps the newcomer." I thought that sounded too much like what my father would say when he was giving me a whipping: "This hurts me more than it hurts you." Sure, sure.

As far as I could tell, sponsorship was yet another form of authority. I liked it and hated it that way. I wanted a sponsor to give me all the "right" answers to my problems and the problems of the world, but I would buck against him whenever he gave me unsolicited or undesired advice.

That thinking pretty much determined the kind of sponsor I became during my second year. I was an authoritarian sponsor in spite of the fact that during my eighth or ninth month I met a guy whose words, actions, and manner consistently demonstrated a sponsorship style which transcended the authority/subservient presumption. That man is my sponsor today. But I learned how to be a sponsor like he is from my sponsees at least as much as I learned from him.

I worked with some newcomers during my second year. I tried to use fear, guilt, and a drill sergeant's voice to motivate them. I gave each one reading assignments from Conference-approved literature, writing assignments, and lots and lots of lectures. I would never share from my own experience, weakness, and despair because that might tarnish my authority in their eyes.

But I did welcome one really struggling newcomer to my apartment for two days. He wanted to stay longer but I insisted that he find his own place; this turned out to be good for us both. I insisted that another call me each day from rehab. That kept the memory so green for me. Meanwhile, giving all those reading assignments kept me really busy. I had to reread all the literature I had assigned so that I could answer any sponsees' questions "perfectly" like a true authority. That's how being a sponsor began to help me.

Two of the guys fired me. Boy, what a blow to my ego. I hoped that they would find other sponsors but was secretly glad to be free of them. At least, that's what I said. One dropped me, I think, because I never opened up to him. He said I never admitted to him that I "made mistakes, too." The other told me that I was constantly criticizing him without complimenting his small steps in the right direction.

Boy, were they both right! But I didn't drink over being wrong and those two guys are still sober. So, by the grace of God, is the one who didn't fire me. It was a tough competition between God and me to see which of us was the true sponsor for these guys, but it was never close. The God of our understanding got each one of us through.

Sponsoring began to work for me later. I prayed to God to let me give more service during my third year. I knew I needed that in order to maintain my sobriety. At that time, I no longer had any sponsees. Within hours of praying for a chance to serve, God presented me with an interim sponsee. We hit it off immediately. Listening had become a lot easier for me. I tried new ways of making firm suggestions. After all, this would be a learning experience for me, too. More frequently than not, I considered the fragile feelings of my sponsee before biting off his head. I tried to toss out possibilities and suggestions without the tone of someone laying down the law. But when I knew in my gut that he needed to hear a blunt message, I gave it to him straight. Finally, and most importantly, I think, I began to share with him what I had previously only shared with my sponsor: what was going on with me. I became vulnerable. And I didn't pick up a drink, a day at a time.

I have learned many lessons from my current sponsee and from the former ones who are still in touch with me from time to time. Try sponsorship. It works.

ROBERT P.
New York, New York

Live and Let Live (Excerpt)

June 2002

One of the wonderful things about our Fellowship is that there is somebody for everybody and we usually seek out people who seem to be a good fit. All of us in AA have a right to our own opinion, even if that opinion is that somebody else's opinion is not as good as ours. There is not a society on earth that places greater emphasis on the individual's right to think, say, and do what he or she pleases than AA. The whole structure of AA is based on a democratic spirit. There are no bosses or gurus. Nowhere on earth do we find such a wonderful society, extending so much freedom to so many people. If it works, don't fix it. We have grown from two people to two million, and we show no signs of getting smaller. We must be doing something right.

JIM N.
West Springfield, Massachusetts

What a Sponsor Is and Is Not

September 2004

The opportunity to help another alcoholic work the Steps and live in the solution keeps me in the heart of what recovery is all about. It has helped me to feel a "part of"—something I had tried to do for years. But it turned out to be as simple as sharing my experience, strength, and hope with another drunk.

The Twelve Steps have the answers to all of the riddles life throws at me. Other drunks took the time to show me, not only by sharing their time and lives, but by living in the solution and dealing with whatever came along with faith and trust. This truly is attraction versus promotion. The "winners" worked the Steps and stayed involved in service—those were the people I wanted to hang out with; that is where I looked for a sponsor.

Today, I sponsor five women who are five reasons for my growth. I met four of these women in a Step meeting—the same meeting that laid the foundation of the Steps for me. I think that spending time at the same Step meeting listening to people share and getting to know them is the place to look for a sponsor. The Steps offer the solutions, and that was what I was looking to learn.

Spiritual fitness is required if I am to be of service to anyone. Without a connection to my Higher Power, I am the same old person with the same old defects, causing the same old pain in my life and others'. So often I have found myself at a complete loss of thought and words for a sponsee who is struggling with life, and then an intuitive thought comes to me and offers a new perspective for consideration. When I wonder where the thought came from, I feel the warmth in my heart, and I know that once again God has done for me what I can't do myself.

As a sponsor, I neither expect nor desire to make decisions for people. I just ask some extra questions about motives, honesty, and spiritual contact. I was taught to make informed decisions and stand ready to accept responsibility for those decisions. I was also taught that Steps Six and Seven come into play when fear is running those decisions. This was a big factor for me when I first started sponsoring—fear that I would mess it up and harm someone as well as the fear that I wouldn't know the "answers" and be viewed as a dope.

Thank God that today I have a clearer perspective on what my role as a sponsor is and isn't. It is to stay sober, be available to listen, share my thoughts, pray for others, and let them live their own lives. It is not to "fix" anyone, get them sober, make them happy, demand they conform, or make their decisions.

My God has blessed me with some incredible role models in sponsors and friends. What a lesson in humility and gratitude sponsorship has given me. I have grown so much in this program and in life. The Promises have come so true in my life—all from cleaning house, trusting God, and working with others.

HILARY T.
Berlin, Connecticut

God's Rolling Stone (From Dear Grapevine)

December 1996

I started going to AA meetings twenty-five years ago in Dearborn, Michigan; I moved to Denver and then on to Phoenix, and back to Michigan. I am God's rolling stone. Each time I moved I gained a friend in a strange city by volunteering to be a sponsor.

I'm now seventy-four years old and I have a dear friend in my latest sponsee. We have a meeting every Sunday at the hotel. I believe that sponsorship is the key to maintaining success in AA.

LIBBY M.
Brownstown, Michigan

Off the Beaten Path (Excerpt)

March 2008

I sobered up as a teenager and my experiences with sponsorship have been a little off the beaten path.

Like many who sobered up young, I know what it's like to be the youngest person in the room and have the most time sober, yet still be considered "inexperienced." As a result, most of my sponsorship experience has been with very young women, as young as thirteen years old. They were the only ones who would give me a real chance. Thank God I found these girls and could carry the AA message to them. They have saved my life.

My first sponsee was a thirteen-year-old girl; I twelfth-stepped her at the request of her school counselor. She used to call me, upset because some guy she thought she could trust had come on to her—often someone over twice her age. I hated to tell her that she wasn't always safe in AA, but it was the harsh truth. I did my best to look out for her and keep her safe, as was done for me.

Through many painful learning experiences, I tried to help her take inventory and change her behavior to be less inviting to such advances. It was trial and error for me as well—I had to learn what was and what was not appropriate for me to do as her sponsor. I wasn't alone in feeling protective of her. There were a number of people who looked out for her safety within the rooms of AA.

She was the first of many young women I have had the gift of working with and this issue has come up with many of them.

I have stumbled my way through many sticky situations without any real guidelines. Finally, I have come to a point where I feel I can handle these situations without so much confusion and self-doubt. I have figured out what I am comfortable with and what feels right according to AA Traditions and principles.

ANONYMOUS

No Absolutes In AA (From Dear Grapevine)

August 2003

There are no absolutes in AA. I just celebrated eight years of sobriety and I've never had a sponsor. I go to meetings, have a strong support group, and talk to someone when I have a problem that seems overwhelming. This is not to say I don't believe in sponsorship, but I do believe that it is not for everyone and that not everyone feels the need to have a sponsor.

At almost every meeting I've gone to, it is rarely suggested that a newcomer get a sponsor; it's more of a command: "Get a sponsor!" I've also heard it said: "If you don't have a sponsor, you're going to drink." Who made up that rule? Because I choose not to have an individual sponsor but to use many people in AA, AA itself, and, of course, my HP as my guides in sobriety, does not mean that I am more likely to pick up than someone who uses an individual sponsor.

It's really a bit frightening: Although I've only been coming around eight years, there seems to have been a shift in AA from suggestions/directions to absolutes. Sharing experience, strength, and hope doesn't mean, to me, setting down a rigid command that must be followed. I will continue to go to AA. It's giving me life. The least I can do is pass it on with the suggestions that were given to me, including the suggestion to find a sponsor, if that's the road the newcomer needs to follow.

JIM H.
Dunmore, Pennsylvania

Tough Sponsor (From Dear Grapevine)

December 2004

Like the author of "The Sponsorship Broker" (September 2004), I do not feel sponsors need to know all the answers, but I think they should know the right questions to ask. I think that a good sponsor knows how to listen. I hear members saying that they had a tough sponsor when they first came in and the key word is always "had." We usually outgrow that sort of sponsorship. Let us just keep telling our story, one alcoholic talking to another alcoholic, and we can literally become miracle workers.

DAVE S.
Prince Albert, Saskatchewan

Finding the Right Fit

May 2003

My first sponsor was what some might call a bully. She ridiculed my thinking, called me names, yelled at me, and occasionally hung up on me when I called. This sponsor had about twenty-five years of sobriety and knew everything. It was her way or the highway, and little of it had anything to do with the Big Book. She sponsored many other women who were also afraid of her, but even more afraid of being ostracized from the group if they left. But after three months of sobriety, I left anyway. That kind of sponsorship simply didn't work for me. And I did feel the social stigma of it from the group, so for a while I left it, too.

I then found a Big Book sponsor, who took the time to sit down with me several nights a week and walk me through the first 164 pages of the Big Book. She explained things to me, helped me with my Fourth Step, and shared all she knew about the program of AA, including its kit of spiritual tools. I was not very close to this person, but felt relaxed and at-ease with her. It was more of a student-teacher relationship, and I will forever be grateful to her for getting me started on the Steps.

When I was ten months sober, this sponsor moved away, so I went back to the group where I originally got sober. For several months, I just went to meetings and didn't get a sponsor. Finally, I told the group I needed help finding one. They hooked me up. The sponsor I have today is about ten years sober. She is a great listener. She encourages me to share and often laughs with me at the way I think. She told me when I first met her, "A sponsor cannot keep you sober. Only a God of your understanding can do that. But I will do anything I can to help you."

Today I thank God for his gift of a wonderful sponsor who encourages me to learn on my own, making full use of the entire Fellowship.

C. H.
San Angelo, Texas

The Spirit of Sponsorship (From Dear Grapevine)

December 2001

My sponsor of over twenty years died two years ago and although I couldn't be with her physically, I was there in thought and spirit.

What made her so special? Perhaps it was her enduring love and enthusiasm for the AA program. Or maybe it was her unshakable belief that all people are inherently good and contribute something positive to life. All I know is what this woman did for me as a frightened newcomer and what she continued to do for the next twenty years.

When I questioned the meaning of life's peaks and valleys, she told me that the secret of life was simply to live it. When I became resentful at someone in AA, she advised me to listen to the message, not the messenger. She taught me to look for miracles in unlikely places and to make myself available to appreciate them.

That's why I love a story her family told me when they returned from scattering her ashes on the sea. She loved the ocean and always said that after she died, she wanted to come back as a dolphin. When they released her ashes, her husband and children saw two dolphins swimming beside them.

"Look!" one of them shouted. "There goes Mom, and she already has a new sponsee."

LYNN C.
South Deerfield, Massachusetts

CHAPTER FOUR

ALL YOU HAVE TO DO IS ASK

Getting past the initial fear of seeking out a sponsor, or becoming a sponsor

AA literature assures us that sponsorship often helps the sponsor more than the sponsee—and only our Higher Powers can keep us sober. Even so, becoming a sponsor can be a scary prospect, especially when it's easy to believe that if you "fail," a person may drink again. "He asked if I could be his sponsor," writes the author of "Any Lengths—Even Brooklyn." "Immediately I felt tiny, 'less-than,' unworthy and an outright fraud."

From the other half of the coin, an AA just beginning to search for a sponsor feels his or her own anxiety. The author of "Will You Fire Me?" writes that he "came to think that if I asked someone to sponsor me, I'd be told no. I developed a terrible fear of rejection."

The fear of the unknown, the fear of screwing up, or the fear of being rejected can keep an AA from sponsoring someone or from asking someone else to sponsor him. The members telling their stories in this chapter talk about moving beyond that fear and just saying "yes."

Will You Fire Me?

March 1997

When I first became sober, I thought I was one of those rare people in AA that wouldn't need a sponsor. I also came to think that if I asked someone to sponsor me, I'd be told no. I developed a terrible fear of rejection. So I held on by my fingernails for seven months. At this time, I felt like I was going crazy. I wasn't working any sort of a program. I knew that if I was to stay sober, I would have to try this sponsor thing.

The first person I asked did just what I'd feared—he rejected me. It hurt to be rejected, but I knew I wanted to stay sober. I only knew two things about the next person I asked—his name and that I'd seen him pick up a chip for five years of sobriety. He accepted me and started me off on the basics of an AA program. He told me to read the Big Book to page 164, then told me to read this a second time, and we'd talk about it. He also had me read a daily devotion book and pray each day to a Higher Power. The last thing he said was to call him every day if I wanted him to sponsor me. I didn't want to do this at the age of fifty-two, but I told him yes, and I did.

One day I called him seven times. I asked him if he would fire me if I called again that day. He laughed and said no. He said I was helping him. I didn't understand this at the time. I know now that he needed me. I'm now four years sober in this God-given miracle of AA, and I still have this loving sponsor. He guides me with his gentle but firm hand. I know that I couldn't have stayed sober without this man. I thank the God of my understanding for him. If you don't have a sponsor, I strongly suggest you get one. This disease of alcoholism kills.

JOE A.
Lexington, South Carolina

Any Lengths—Even Brooklyn

September 2010

I trekked out to Brooklyn tonight.

A classmate of mine had mentioned not being able to "touch that stuff" when alcohol was mentioned. After class (and summoning some courage) I asked if he went to meetings.

"You mean, Alcoholics Anonymous meetings?" he said, in apparent shock that I was asking that question. He affirmed he did, and had been sober for six months. Before parting, however, he leveled with me and said he only had one day back. I offered my phone number, and we made a plan to make a meeting in his area.

Brooklyn would be a trying journey because I live in Queens and it was rush hour. But with three years of sobriety, I felt up to the task. I plodded through an hour-and-a-half of traffic, but I found the church and my classmate, and was on time to boot. We sat through two meetings; I shared during the second one. As we walked outside, he asked for a ride. While I was driving, he asked if I could be his sponsor. In nearly three-and-a-half years of sobriety and making meetings very regularly, only one other person had asked me to sponsor him; and had disappeared soon after. I accepted.

Immediately I felt tiny, "less-than," unworthy and an outright fraud. I told him my sponsor and I weren't doing enough work, and that he should know that. I also said to not drink, and to call me. I could think of nothing else.

After I dropped him off, I instinctively called a fellow alcoholic who, along with his wife, had a very strong foundation in the program. I told him of my dilemma: I didn't know what to do. He said, "Why not suggest he go to meetings, call you every day and start reading the Big Book?" Hmm—why didn't I think of that? I also explained my own sponsor problems, and he agreed to help me out.

In effect, he became my new sponsor.

With the helping hand of AA, I now find myself with a new sponsor and sponsee. And it's a beautiful thing! In AA, I've discovered that there is no shame in asking for help, and that in doing so, in simply asking, we help others.

My new sponsor was grateful to hear from me, I from him, my classmate from me, and we all helped each other stay sober, together.

ADAM K.
Queens, New York

Need a Sponsor? Who, Me?

January 1975

Being asked to be someone's sponsor is not an opportunity to play God. It is, rather, a humbling experience, in which it behooves the sponsor to pray for guidance. It also involves a great deal of listening. Empathy, not sympathy or pity, is the most useful quality a sponsor can cultivate.

SALLY H.
Bellevue, Washington

A Bigger God

March 2002

I recently asked a newcomer, "Have you gotten a sponsor yet?" She said no. "How do you do that?" I told her all you have to do is ask.

"Okay, how about you?" she said. "Will you be my sponsor?"

For a split second, I forgot to breathe. I didn't mean me. She needed a sponsor with a lot of time, someone with more than a measly three years. And then I heard myself say, "I'd love to sponsor you." It just slipped out. Now I was really in trouble. I'm not a sponsor, I'm a sponsee. I don't have time to sponsor someone else;

I have to work my own Steps.

The next thing I knew, I was talking about reading the Big Book. I must have been coherent because she seemed pleased when we parted ways, me telling her exactly what my sponsor had told me, "Call even if you have nothing to say. It's like a fire drill—you want to be in practice when there's an emergency."

I beat myself up on the ride home. Couldn't I have come up with something more original to tell her? "Call even if you have nothing to say!" It sounded so ... well, sponsor-ish! I'd hated making those calls in the beginning, those "Hi, I'm just checking in" messages I left on my sponsor's answering machine.

I'm afraid of change. Afraid of progress without perfection. It's always been this way. I sat down and I prayed. I prayed for the willingness to be the best sponsor I'm capable of being. All I have to do is share my experience, strength, and hope. I got out my Big Book and began reading from the beginning.

I've been a sponsor now for all of four days, but it feels as if I've been through a century of spiritual growth. I'm definitely an inch or two taller. Because of this subtle shift in perception about myself, the shift from working the Steps as a sponsee to working the Steps as a sponsor, I'm bursting out of my seams.

When I'm in fear, my sponsor always tells me, "Maybe you should get a bigger God." This used to dumbfound me, but I get it now. The longer I stay sober, the fuller my life gets, and my God expands accordingly. Instead of protecting what I have, I've taken to staying open. "Open, open, open," as one of my sober friends likes to coach herself. This week, I find myself on a moment to moment basis, asking God, "What's next?"

STEFANI R.
Los Angeles, California

Fledgling Sponsor (From Dear Grapevine)

March 2009

I remember asking my sponsor, "When do I start the Steps?" He replied, "When do you want to get well?"

I was sober only four months when I met a new friend at the eight o'clock meeting. He was just like me, a hopeless case willing to do anything to find sobriety. When he asked me for help, I quickly called my sponsor. He said, "Take him by the hand and guide him as I guide you." We walked to meetings, prayed, read the Big Book and took the Twelve Steps together, with my sponsor's help.

One day at a time has turned into seven years. We're no longer homeless or hopeless, thanks to AA. It's really about one drunk reaching out to another.

DAVID M.
Martinsville, Virginia

Cross Talk Wisdom (From Dear Grapevine)

July 2007

Recent stories about "cross talk" brought to mind something that happened to me at a meeting in Catlett, Virginia, over twenty years ago when I was new and struggling to stay sober.

I raised my hand to report that I had had another slip. I then went on talking for several more minutes about how dismayed and astonished I was. I was carrying the proverbial "mess," not the message. Finally, the leader, a fellow named Dick, held up his hand and stopped me with a pointed question: What had my sponsor said when I called him and told him I wanted to drink?

Within a few days, I had gotten my first sponsor. I'm sure that the other people at the meeting were thankful that Dick interrupted me. I remain thankful to this day. I'm glad he cared more about my life than he did about my feelings.

MARBURY W.
Greenbelt, Maryland

A Helping Hand

January 1997

I met the woman who was to become my sponsor when I had nine days. I forgot what she said that night, but I got the sense that this lady had her head on straight. I called her on day twelve because I didn't know what else to do. She told me she had other plans that night, but surprised me by showing up at my meeting. There were no chairs left, so I sat on the floor and she sat on the floor, too. When the meeting was over, I asked her to be my sponsor. She hugged me and said, "God sent you to me!" She has been my sponsor ever since and is one of the most important people in my life.

When I achieved one year sober, we both started looking for someone I could sponsor, so that I could share the experience of sponsorship from the other side of the table. At first I looked for newcomers, asked them if they had a sponsor and if not, I'd be happy to be their sponsor. No luck. A man with several years told me that approach probably scared or intimidated them, so I backed off.

If there was a newcomer at a meeting, I'd give my phone number to her and say I'd be happy to help in any way I could. No pressure. No luck either. I signed up in several interim sponsorship books. No luck. I sometimes acted as beginner's liaison in my home group. Again, no luck.

Finally, my sponsor met a woman just out of rehab and told me to talk with her, take her out for coffee, and maybe I could be her sponsor. I did what my sponsor told me to do. After a few weeks, the woman did ask me to sponsor her, but rarely called. Wanting to be helpful, I called her. After a few weeks of this, I asked her to call me. She stopped calling completely.

Pretty soon we would just hook up at a meeting and go out for coffee or a quick bite to eat. After another couple of weeks she wouldn't make it to the meeting, but would want to go out to the coffee shop. Again, I suggested she call, because I needed time to share with my friends, and offered to set aside a time every week when she and I could get together in person. She stopped coming to the same meetings I went to and we didn't go out for coffee. Eventually, I told her I couldn't be her sponsor anymore. I had to break this news over her answering machine because she didn't return my calls to her office.

My feelings were hurt and my expectations too high. Nothing I can say or do can control another's behavior. Here is a prime application for the slogan "Live and Let Live," which reminds me that the only goal is to be helpful.

Months passed. I'd still give out my phone number at meetings and act as liaison, but no one asked me to be a sponsor. Pretty soon, women whom I'd watched counting days had one or two sponsees. My sponsor even got another sponsee.

Recently, a woman who hadn't had a drink in four days came to my home group. I asked if she wanted to go out for coffee and she said yes. She was asking a lot of questions about sponsorship and I offered to be her sponsor. She said that she would like that, if it wasn't too much trouble. No trouble at all, I replied, but please try to call me before two in the morning.

No calls. I'd see her at meetings and ask how things were going. She'd be eager to share with me in person but reluctant to pick up the phone. A week later I saw her run out of a meeting. I followed and asked if she was okay. She was agitated. She told me she had been calling another woman in the program every day and that she was working on the First Step with her. She had a sponsor, but it wasn't me.

While I'm disappointed I don't have a sponsee, I feel joy in doing the Twelfth Step work that I do. I speak at meetings. I still give out my phone number. My name is still in the sponsorship books at groups around town. I've been on Twelfth Step calls. I act as liaison when called upon, and I'm secretary and treasurer of my home group. I enjoy going to a coffee shop with others after meetings. I say hello to new folks, and make a special effort to remember their names. Several of those people, whom I met when they were still shaking and sweating out the booze, are sober now for more than a year. They remember that I looked them in the eye, said welcome, and extended my hand in fellowship.

As a sponsee, I'm joyous. As a sponsor, I'm perplexed. Maybe I'll never be a sponsor, but that won't stop me from extending my hand and saying welcome.

ELIZABETH H.
New York, New York

CHAPTER FIVE

GOING TO ANY LENGTHS

Saying yes to sponsoring a troubled or mentally challenged newcomer

The author of "This Sponsor Makes House Calls" has one sponsee in jail, another in the hospital for manic depression, and a third who's hungover after deciding to pick up a drink. "I told [my sponsor] that I didn't think I had the hang of this sponsorship thing yet," he writes. "My sponsor pointed out that in sponsorship, as in all Twelfth Step work, our primary job is to carry the message of sobriety. I had been doing just that all day."

"Work with Phil has made all the difference. He's helped me through the worst of the agony," the author of "Mentally Ill" writes. The AAs in this chapter, such as the one sponsoring a mentally ill man, made choices to try to help particularly troubled fellow members, and in doing so stayed sober themselves.

A Sponsor's Sadness

March 1991

I came into AA in 1984 with a crushed spirit, both mentally and physically ill. Slowly, I began to clear up. My health improved, my mental state seemed reasonably sound, and my spirit healed. I got a sponsor and learned from him the ins and outs of the AA way of life. I attended Step, Big Book, speaker and discussion meetings. I made coffee, swept floors, emptied ashtrays, read the secretary's report. My life slowly came together.

At some point in my fourth year of sobriety, I began to feel the need to give something back. I had been asked a few times to sponsor people but I always declined, feeling I wasn't ready. Now I agreed to temporarily sponsor someone I had seen at meetings. We lived fairly close to each other and often drove to meetings together.

What began as a mutually satisfying relationship soon turned sour. My new friend's demands upon my time seemed unreasonable. There were calls three or four times a day and appearances at my door whenever the mood struck. I kept telling myself that Bill and Dr. Bob put up with this kind of thing. They even had people living with them. No inconvenience was, it seemed to me, too great for them. What was wrong with me? Why was I getting so resentful?

It turned out that my friend had problems other than alcohol. She had manic depressive illness. She never hid this from me, but we never discussed it either. She didn't want to talk about it and I didn't want to hear.

The inevitable came to pass and a psychotic manic depressive episode occurred. It was violent and destructive. Try as I might, with all my solid AA background, I could not help her. She was removed from her home by the police after twenty-four terrible hours. My heart broke for her.

She was now tied down in a mental hospital, expecting me to get her out. I was still terrified at the scene I had just witnessed. I knew fear that day I had never known in all my years of drinking. As it turned out, this episode was one of many similar ones she had had. Her family assured me she would be fine given time and the right medication.

I was filled with fear. I lost sleep and became physically ill. My answer came after talking with my sponsor: I had to detach with love. I was powerless but I never really accepted that. Deep in my heart I felt if I really tried hard enough I could swing things to the way I wanted.

In my ignorance about her illness, I may have even hurt her by not recognizing the signs that were becoming more and more obvious. I kept trying harder, she kept getting sicker.

I have two reasons for writing this. First, someone else may learn from my sadness. AA works for problems with alcohol, but it has no power to arrest manic depressive illness. Second, if and when I try to sponsor someone again, I'll be sure we discuss alcoholism. My former sponsee and I never did talk about drinking. That sounds strange to say now, but it's true. We talked and talked about kids, husbands, meetings, houses, and so on—but not alcoholism or the program.

There are many things in this world I am powerless over, many situations I cannot fix. I would do well to remember that. I can't, God can, so I think I'll let him.

J. N. W.
Lynn, Massachusetts

Kindred Spirits

March 2009

I have been sober in Alcoholics Anonymous for 20 years. I got sober in the Westside Alano Club on Pico Boulevard in Los Angeles. It was within walking distance of the mental hospital where I had been spending the Social Security Administration's money. They had a program for people with psychiatric diagnoses in addition to chemical dependencies.

I was depressed and pretty psychotic. I just wanted to feel like I was okay. I wanted to feel like everybody wasn't always staring at me or like the world really wasn't going to crash down on top of me.

I wanted to feel like maybe I was worth liking, like maybe there was something good coming down the road for me someday. They tried every kind of pill they had, but none of them seemed to do the trick. Nor did the shock treatments.

Alcohol was the only thing that really seemed to work for me. I've heard people in AA call alcohol "liquid courage," and it sure was that for me in the beginning.

I drank and smoked my way through high school, had my first vacation at a psych hospital when I was 19 and landed myself in a locked ward in restraints by the time I was 23. I hung myself with a bed sheet in a door jamb and lost consciousness.

I was found, cut down and given an emergency tracheotomy. When I awoke from the coma a few days later, I was paralyzed on my left side and didn't know my own name. After numerous MRIs they determined that I had killed at least 10 percent of my brain. I was expected to be disabled for the rest of my life.

Fortunately, my dad and my doctor had higher expectations. I had physical therapy to learn to walk again and when I was released from the hospital some months later, I was sent to a rehab.

But that's not the important part of my story. The important part is how I got to Alcoholics Anonymous. There was a man in my hospital therapy group who befriended me. Stan somehow found me to be a kindred spirit and started taking me to his AA meetings. He taught me the importance of looking for similarities instead of differences.

Eventually, I did the stuff you told me, though not very willingly. I had a chip on my shoulder about everything. It took me a long time to find a home group I felt comfortable in and a sponsor I could relate to.

The woman I finally chose to be my sponsor, Marla H. from Redondo Beach, didn't put up with any self-pity from me and when I whined about my psychiatric problems she lovingly replied that "the Twelve Steps will work for anyone—even the likes of me or you—if they are worked honestly. So stop whining and get to it."

In recovery I have found a new way to live. Marla was right when she told me that if I did the Steps and stuck around here, the quality of my problems would improve. I used to have to do things like figure out how to get the bus to the welfare office, and now I have to arrange for lodging for the many relatives who will be attending my college graduation in June.

I have found joys in life I never thought possible, and I've also endured things in sobriety that I never thought I could live through. I've heard people say in these rooms that AA is a selfish program, and I so dislike hearing that.

My selfishness is what gets me in the most trouble, and the Steps talk about selfishness and self-centeredness being at the root of our problems. I like to say that AA is a program you can use to learn to follow the will of your higher self.

The basic principles of our program—honesty, open-mindedness, and willingness—when applied to a life lived in service to God and our fellows, have the power to transform not only the lives of alcoholics, but possibly the world around us as well.

PAM P.
San Pedro, California

This Sponsor Makes House Calls

March 1982

About a year and a half after I had my last drink, I was still very active and going to a lot of meetings; but Sunday, with its drink signals, was still a tough day for me. Fortunately, I live in New York City and have meetings available all day Sunday.

One day, I received a call from a fellow I had gotten sober with. He had recently picked up a drink, had beaten up his girlfriend, and was in jail awaiting trial. The following Sunday, I started very early on the two-hour trip to the jail with a few personal things, a Big Book, and a copy of the Grapevine. After sharing with my friend my opinion that it wasn't his girlfriend or the judge who had landed him in the pokey, but the first drink, I headed back to New York for a noontime meeting.

Later that day, I dropped by a local hospital to visit a sponsee of mine who had signed himself in for treatment of manic depression after having been sober a year. It felt a bit strange, being in a locked ward for the first time, but it proved the old saying that anywhere two alcoholics get together to talk about recovery, it's a meeting.

After the hospital, I decided to drop in on another pigeon. (I'm the kind of sponsor who makes house calls!) When I phoned, I was told he had gotten drunk the night before. After taking my hung-over friend to a meeting, I went home to call my own sponsor for some advice.

I told him that I didn't think I had the hang of this sponsorship thing yet. Here I was, having just visited two persons I was sponsoring and one who called me his sponsor, but I didn't have one healthy member to my name. One was in jail; one was in the nuthouse; and one was hungover. What was I doing wrong?

First, my sponsor pointed out that in sponsorship, as in all

Twelfth Step work, our primary job is to carry the message of sobriety. I had been doing just that all day. He then asked how I felt right at that moment. I told him I felt just great. And that, he said, was the other purpose of sponsorship—to make the sponsor feel just great.

ANONYMOUS
Bronx, New York

Mentally Ill

March 2010

Polyester can set his skin afire. Voices assault him. He bangs his head against the walls to silence them. The voices retaliate; inflict pain internally and externally. The antipsychotic medication he's on has turned him into a type 2 diabetic. He's excruciatingly lonely; constantly marginalized. People are reflexively friendly toward him—but rarely extend themselves beyond a handshake and a smile. Seldom, if ever, do they invite him out to coffee or over for a meal.

Phil is mentally ill.

When he asked me to sponsor him last year, my reaction was typically arrogant: I'm too good for this. I'm 30 years sober; I should be sponsoring movie stars.

I was going through the most painful period of my sobriety. I'd split with my wife. I'd married her late in life. I'd waited for the right one. I was sure of it. Before I'd proposed, I'd prayed for signs, gotten them, given up my place on the beach in Santa Monica and moved to Canada.

Meetings in suburban Toronto were not the same as Santa Monica. I preferred the raucous effervescence of the West Coast—but I had more or less resigned myself to the difference. Shortly after the wedding, I got in a philosophical dispute with an old-timer.

It was so earth-shattering that I can't remember what it was about. But it was the excuse I needed to do something I thought I'd never do: quit AA. I didn't need it anymore. It was an effective path—but I'd outgrown it. I'd heard it all: the cliches, the self-obsession, the ignorant group-speak. It was unhealthy for someone as spiritually advanced as me to continue. It was time to graduate.

I'd come down with chronic fatigue syndrome. I was exhausted and cranky a good deal of the time. The longer I stayed away from meetings, the worse it got. Untreated alcoholism is a prescription for self-obsession. I had no idea how hard I was being on my wife.

I was fine, or so I kept telling myself. I was meditating three hours a day, delivering books for the library, visiting the elderly in nursing homes. I was even mentoring a grade school boy, and considering becoming his Big Brother. My spiritual condition was being fully addressed. Wasn't it? Then why was this woman who had adored me kicking me out? How had I trashed the most nurturing life I'd ever known?

Here was Phil—fresh from a mental institution, heavily medicated, more than a few steps removed from reality—asking me to sponsor him. I couldn't help him. I wasn't a shrink. What did I know about the intricacies of mental illness? Besides, I was too busy, too important.

I'd been sober long enough to know better. God had always given me exactly what I needed to get through difficult times. But this time I was convinced it was different. I'd turned my back on the program that had saved my life. I'd destroyed a marriage and wounded a woman I professed to adore. I was a complete idiot. I didn't deserve help.

I was so down I couldn't see how a guy like Phil—this depressed, this troubled—could be anything but a burden. Conversations were monosyllabic, halting at best. It felt wrong. So I did the bare minimum: rides to meetings, the occasional coffee or dinner. I was doing both of us a disservice. He was suffering far more than I was, and I was keeping him at arm's length. I was getting nothing out of it because I was putting nothing into it. God was supplying the glue I needed to put my shattered self back together—but I was refusing to squeeze the tube.

Recently in meditation I had an epiphany. I was struggling to overcome the side effects of this illness—gut pain and frayed concentration, trying to keep a straight back—and was about to give up when I begged God: "Please help me ignore the pain and feel closer to you."

The answer shot back (or at least I thought it did): "If you want me, you must mean it." I gritted my teeth, sat straighter and mustered all the love I could manage. Within minutes the pain diminished, my concentration returned, and I was drenched in a waterfall of grace.

Not long afterward, I took Phil to a meeting. His blood sugar spiked. He couldn't sit still. He was sweating, squirming, panting. His voices launched a full-scale assault. It drove him out of the meeting in tears. I suddenly realized that no matter how bad I had it, no matter how hard it was to be with him, if I was to be his sponsor, I had to mean it. I had to go to "any lengths."

I started taking him for long walks, concerts, real meals. In no time, the burden lifted and a genuine friendship blossomed. Monosyllables turned into sentences, sentences into conversations. We started to laugh—a lot. I suggested he get a bike. He was thrilled with the newfound freedom, the endorphin-inducing exercise. I was gratified to see him transformed from a parchment-colored zombie to a tanned dude. Everyone has been commenting on how well he looks.

In a way, I was the one who was mentally ill. I was cheating myself out of God's grace, the grace that envelops us when we walk into the prison to carry the message or shake the hand of the man quivering on the bed in the darkened fetid room. That same grace surrounds the mentally ill in abundance.

Just because they're on meds doesn't mean they don't suffer as much as I do. Just because they're one step removed from my reality, doesn't mean the Steps won't work for them. Was I in tune with reality when I walked in the doors?

Not only has Phil been lifted up by doing a second Fourth and Fifth Step, he's become a Tenth Step pro. He's channeling his mental illness into wellness: writing down his fears on a regular basis, and reading them to me. He's begun to march, admitting difficulties and defects that only months ago he'd denied.

It's still one drunk talking to another. So what if when there are only two of us in the room, three or four voices are clamoring to be recognized? All of us get to feel better.

Work with Phil has made all the difference. He's helped me through the worst of the agony. Sure, it's tough some days. I get down on myself for bowing out on the program, and for my inability to overcome this physical illness, to minimize my character defects and to rise above. I miss my wife and I'm terribly lonely—but none of it cuts as deeply as it did. If it does, I know what to do. Pick up the phone and call Phil.

DUANE T.
Hamilton, Ontario

CHAPTER SIX

NO GUARANTEES

The heartache of losing a beloved sponsor or sponsee

"When it seems like love just isn't enough, I remind myself that it is all I have to give beyond my experience, strength and hope. For some people, love may not be enough," writes the author of "Beyond My Reach," after a sponsee decides to start drinking again and dies.

And it's not always the sponsee who picks up. "I could not believe that the man who had brought me through the Steps into a new way of life had drunk again. I felt lied to and betrayed," the author of "When My Sponsor Drank," writes. "In the end, I realized I hadn't been betrayed at all. Instead, I had learned the important lesson that none of us are guaranteed a lifetime of sobriety."

The bond of sponsorship can be very tight, and losing a beloved sponsor or sponsee to alcohol or to death is heartbreaking. These stories illustrate using the program to deal with the loss and continuing to live sober.

Beyond My Reach

May 2009

I love working with young people, even though I didn't get sober until I was in my 40s. I deal with my regret over being drunk for so many years by helping others get—and stay—sober before they drink away a large chunk of their lives. It makes sense to me. God keeps putting young people in my path; they keep asking me to sponsor them. And I keep saying yes. It seems to work most of the time. However, I cannot help but wonder about many whom I have not heard from again—yet.

One man had asked me to be his sponsor when he was 19. He showed great promise and was progressing well—things looked very bright indeed—until the day he told me he had decided he didn't have a drinking problem and he was leaving the program. My heart sank, for I had heard his story. He might not have known, but I did. The Big Book says, "We do not like to pronounce any individual as alcoholic." It doesn't say I can't, or don't know how. And in his case, I didn't.

I didn't tell him that he was an alcoholic. I did the only thing I could think to do. I told him to call me—drunk or sober—to keep me posted on how he was doing, that I would always care about him and be there for him when he wanted to get back off the elevator to hell. I told him to remember I wanted to help if he wanted help.

Six months later, I went to his funeral. He was killed in a drunk-driving accident. His family was devastated. I was crushed. The questions spun in my head like a tornado: Had I done all I could do? Should I have called him instead of waiting for him to call me? Should I have contacted his family? Why would God take a 20-year-old when he let me drink for 25 years? Then I remembered something my first sponsor told me.

"You don't get them sober," he said, "God does that. It is only your job to be ready for God to use you as an extension." That helped, but it wasn't enough. This one had hit too close to home.

I took his obituary and had it laminated. I keep it in a prominent place so that I don't forget how easy it is to get back on the elevator—how easy it can be to believe I will be able to ride it down just a few more floors. I want to remember that some elevators are faulty. Their cables can snap and the brakes can fail. They might not provide me with a way to get back off. I may just end up speeding to my death without a single Step in sight.

I want to remember this for me, especially when someone I know decides to go back out. I want him to know I will be here, but he might not get the chance to make another comeback; the first drink might just be his last. I want to love him enough to chew his ear enough to—hopefully—put something in there that might help him change his mind. I want to show him the love I have been shown, because it is through the love that we begin to heal.

When it seems like love just isn't enough, I remind myself that it is all I have to give beyond my experience, strength and hope. For some people, love may not be enough. I hope the story about Jimmy might be. I hope my sponsee didn't die in vain.

MARK E.
Lansing, Michigan

When My Sponsor Drank

February 2009

Like many lessons in sobriety, placing people in AA on pedestals is something that I did not understand the full implications of initially. I had been putting recovering alcoholics on pedestals since before I even got to AA. My dad, for example, had been sober twelve years before I made it to the rooms, and based on his horrendous battle with booze before AA, I was sure he was a walking miracle.

My own sobriety began a number of years later, after many physical, emotional, spiritual, and legal problems with alcohol. At that point, it was suggested I get a sponsor who had been through the Steps and lived a life that I myself wanted to live. I found somebody who seemed to fit that bill, and we soon began a daily dialogue that led to him guiding me through each of the Twelve Steps.

Weeks meshed into months as we saw each other regularly at meetings, reviewed chapters in the book, and traveled to various AA functions around our state. I listened intently to his emphasis on prayer and gratitude as I built my foundation and took a personal inventory. I completed my Fifth Step with him and proceeded through my Eighth and Ninth Steps with the selfless guidance of this man whom I regarded with intense respect and unending praise.

My sponsor and I met weekly as I began to incorporate a daily inventory into my sobriety and listened to him describe his own experience with meditation. Upon reaching the Twelfth Step, my sponsor asked me to look back on the journey we had gone through together and to turn to others to give away what I had received.

I found myself very energetic about sobriety and more than willing to approach newcomers. I began working closely with new men in AA while other areas of my life began to get busy.

That's when I found out my sponsor had picked up a drink.

I was shocked. I could not believe that the man who had brought me through the Steps into a new way of life had drunk again. I felt lied to and betrayed. I had seen people go back to drinking since coming into the program, but in the case of my sponsor, I felt personally sick with frustration and misunderstanding.

After talking with others, I was made aware that sobriety was not guaranteed forever, and I was directed to page 85 of the Big Book, which discusses the daily reprieve we have from alcoholism and how the maintenance of an alcoholic's spiritual condition must take place on a daily basis.

In the end, I realized I hadn't been betrayed at all. Instead, I had learned the important lesson that none of us are guaranteed a lifetime of sobriety and that putting someone on a pedestal can be dangerous for me and for the alcoholic I admire.

It has been over three years since this occurred, and I have tried to remain grateful for each day that I am sober, using the amazing AA principles my sponsor taught me in my first year of sobriety.

DAVID J.
Grand Rapids, Michigan

Every Second Counts

February 1998

I have loved every gal I've ever sponsored and always learned valuable lessons from each of them, none more obvious than the lessons learned from a woman named Rose.

Born Italian and Catholic, Rose was a warm, gregarious person by nature who got sober at fifty. She came to me fresh out of rehab and asked me to be her sponsor. It was obvious she'd taken the First Step and we went through the next two quickly. She was so eager to get on with things so we talked about setting out on her Fourth Step. She called me the following day and we met for lunch. "Am I doing this right?" she asked, pulling a sheaf of handwritten paper out of her purse.

She read and I listened. She had made a mighty beginning. "When did you do all this?" I said. "I thought you had a particularly long day at work yesterday."

"I did," she said, "but this was important and I worked on this instead of having dinner."

I was impressed. She had already covered much of her childhood and early years in school. I explained to her that she also needed sleep and food because she needed to be alert on the job—she was an anesthesiologist.

But there was no slowing her down. She called a few more times for lunch meetings and within a short time we were past the Fifth

Step and working on the character defects which had showed up in the Fourth. Her quest for as much of the AA program as was humanly possible was nearly daunting to me, but I'm stubborn too, and I felt myself growing through all this.

Rose glowed. She had it—there could be no doubt. When she shared in meetings it was as though we were listening to a real old-timer. She said it was because of all the therapy she had been in over the years. We had fun mapping her Eighth and Ninth Step plans.

Then one day she announced she had a new sponsor, a priest. She needed to move ahead spiritually and she wanted more than I could give. I was crushed at first, but after talking this over with my husband (my sponsor in times of dire crisis), I realized that there was nothing I could do about this but let go of Rose. Outwardly accepting, but inwardly seething at times, I finally realized I couldn't be everyone's sponsor and I had other sponsees who needed me.

At meetings we attended together I noticed a palpable change in Rose. Her inner beauty and peace seemed permanently reflected in her countenance. She began to sponsor people. Her children moved to town just to be close to her and one got in a recovery program of his own. Her job took on a new dimension. In short, she became an AA poster child—all this within the space of eighteen months and much of it without my help.

I sulked a bit. My own son was still out there. My finances were a disaster. "Why, God?" I asked. "Why don't I have what Rose has? I've been working five years longer at these things and I've tried to do my best with the Steps." I got no reply.

But I knew that my prayers were tinged with envy, and so I began to pray for Rose as I had prayed for other persons I'd resented.

Then one day the phone rang and it was a friend of mine in the Fellowship who was a nurse in intensive care. "I thought you'd want to know that Rose is here—she's dying. She suffered a massive stroke at work about an hour ago. Her children are here. I can't believe it," she said.

I sat down, stunned, by the phone. I realized that Rose had received what she needed when she needed it. She took a cram course in AA because she didn't have the time to acquire years and years of experience. I delivered a eulogy at her service and said a final goodbye to my friend. I also said goodbye to envy—even of spiritual things.

MINDY S.
LaBelle, Florida

Sponsee Gets Tough (From Dear Grapevine)

September 2007

I have been sober for over twenty years. Getting to AA was the result of hitting bottom—or so I thought. At the eighteen-year mark in my sobriety, I hit an all-time low, sober.

Loss of a business and a marriage almost put me over the top. I quit going to meetings after getting my feelings hurt. I also fired my sponsor and sponsees.

I did point out who I thought would make good sponsors for my sponsees. One sponsee did not seem to be making an effort to get another sponsor, so one day I asked if he had someone in mind. He looked at me and said, "I'm not looking for another sponsor. I am waiting for you to get your act together and come back and finish the job you started."

Well, that sure was a humbling experience for this drunk. It woke me up enough to realize that there is no greater love than what one alcoholic has for another.

BRIAN B.
Astoria, Oregon

One Last Wish

December 2000

I spent my drinking days as a loner and as a woman who did things on her own without following rules or conventions. I carried this approach to life into the beginning of my sobriety. Consequently, I was three years sober before I decided to work the Steps.

By the time I got to Step Five, I realized I couldn't go on any longer without a sponsor. But who could it be? I had spent so much of my life being a lone wolf; I couldn't imagine asking anyone to be my sponsor, let alone admitting my shortcomings.

I searched my home group for a man or woman with whom I might feel comfortable enough to really talk. I was still poor at reaching out and communicating. One night, I decided to ask Ben to be my sponsor and to help me with Step Five. Ben appeared to have just the right amount of understanding, warmth, and humor I was looking for.

He agreed to help me with Step Five and to be my sponsor at least on a temporary basis. Later on in the meeting, Ben was called on to share.

When he spoke, he mentioned something about his state of health that I hadn't known before: Ben had been diagnosed as having AIDS. My first thought was, "Poor Ben has a dreaded disease, and I am expecting him to lend me a helping hand. Maybe I should be the one lending the hand." I hadn't yet learned the principle, "Service is its own reward." I soon understood that Ben was able to help himself a great deal by his constant service to others.

After I had admitted the exact nature of my wrongs to my Higher Power, I made an appointment to discuss them with Ben. I carried on with AA's Steps from there.

The following year, Ben presented me with my four-year cake, and my life within the program continued to grow. I came to rely on Ben's strength, as well as my own and that of other people. Eight months later, I got a call about Ben: He had taken a sudden and rather unexpected turn for the worse. After work the next day, I headed straight for the hospital. From his hospital bed, and in a weak condition, Ben asked how I was coming along with my goals in the program. He was genuinely concerned. Although he would be gone ten days later, Ben's powerful hope for his sponsees, and for all members, was ever-present.

For the first week after my sponsor's death, my only two feelings were sadness and confusion. Then, with the help of others, I remembered Ben's sole wish for me—that I continue within the program, happily. Through his example, I am learning more deeply to live each day and to enjoy life, "one day at a time."

ANONYMOUS
Vancouver, British Columbia

Little Hobo

March 1993

Tired of trying to survive, physically sick from my last drunk, and so financially unstable that I was living in my car in the dead of winter, I stumbled into my first meeting of Alcoholics Anonymous. The building was warm, the coffee was hot and free, and I was scared to death. The room was full of people all talking at once, laughing and hugging each other. My first thought was that probably they didn't get to see each other very often.

While I was trying to make my way to a corner (in order to keep my back covered), a lady came up to me. She told me her name and asked mine. I was so scared that I gave her one of my aliases. She said, "You are the most pathetic-looking piece of human garbage I've ever seen, so come sit with me." I was too afraid to refuse her. She told me, "When they ask for newcomers you stand up and tell them who you are and what you are." When I asked her, "What am I?" she suggested I call myself an alcoholic until we could figure it out.

That started my relationship with Dessie, my first sponsor. After three months of not drinking, going to meetings, and sharing some of my life with her, I finally told her my real name. She laughed and told me what I call myself was not important and from that day on she called me her "Little Hobo," since riding freight trains had been part of my story.

At six months I had a slip and she was right there to get me right back to the meetings. She let me know that she was never ashamed of me or of any of the things I had done or continued to do. Every time I asked her why she kept on loving me, she always replied, "That's what God put me here to do."

During my second attempt at sobriety she helped me to get back in college. She was there for me when my mother died in March, and she cried tears of joy when I graduated with my Bachelor of Science degree in nursing in May. Then tragedy struck.

Just eight days after my graduation, I was going with two other members to give someone a ride to a meeting when an eighteen-wheeler ran over us. My condition was so critical that the only doctor who would take me was in my sponsor's hometown.

Once again she was there for me. For nine months while I was hospitalized she was there every day. My face was destroyed and it took many surgeries to rebuild it. Six months after the wreck the doctors told me I would never be able to be a nurse again due to the physical damage.

I planned what was to be my last drunk. I signed out of the hospital thirty minutes before my sponsor was to pick me up for my weekend pass.

By the time she found me I had been drinking for several hours. She took me home with her and then to a meeting. When I told her how bad I was hurting, she said the words I have never forgotten: "Good! I hope it hurts like hell, because if it hurts enough you will never have to do it again." That was my last drink—November 16, 1982.

In February 1983, my sponsor came over one morning for a cup of coffee and to talk. She said she wanted to tell me in person that the doctors had found cancer and were going to start operating. I was angry at God and she told me, "God did not give me cancer. It is just a part of life. Besides, he only loaned you and me to each other for a while."

The next nine months were a series of surgeries, chemotherapy, and many days and nights sitting outside of ICU waiting to see her for just a few minutes. I made more meetings during that time than any other period of my sobriety.

Two days before I was to celebrate my one year of sobriety I was sitting outside of ICU waiting to visit her when her husband came out. He said, "Dessie and I have talked it over and we have agreed that you can go in and stay with her. We have said our good-byes and now she just wants to be with her 'Little Hobo.'"

I was able to be with her for the next three days until she left us for good. I have trouble writing this even now because of the tears flowing.

The unconditional love which my sponsor gave to me still lives within my heart. To the ladies I am honored to sponsor I pass on the many things which she taught me, and by doing that the circle remains unbroken.

REGINA M.
N. Charleston, South Carolina

Not All Make It Back (From Dear Grapevine)

October 2009

Thank you so much for "Beyond My Reach" (May 2009), by a sponsor whose young sponsee relapses and is killed in a drunk-driving accident.

I, too, sponsor a couple of young people. One of my sponsees came to me and confessed she had relapsed, even after we had talked over and over about old people, places and things. She started pointing out that she was young and could just come back any time.

At that moment the article flashed into my mind. I got my copy, put it in front of her and told her to read it.

Then I handed her a pen and legal pad—so she could write out in her own words what she wanted me to tell her family, friends and fellow AAs if she wasn't able to make it back. They'd all want to know why and I was not going to be without her answer.

After much talking, she now understands having a sponsor means more than telling on yourself after the fact. The article opened both our eyes. Our phones now work both ways most days.

MISS KAY
Murray, Kansas

Unbending Sponsorship (Excerpt)

November 2008

I was holding Ruby Ann's hand when she took her last breath. She was in a nursing facility in Mississippi, her home state. She'd moved to Mississippi a year earlier, even though she had no family or friends left there, to settle her estate. Four months into her stay, she was diagnosed with terminal cancer.

I flew out from California to be with her for a few weeks, to try to be helpful. I was to take five flights more to be with her, one or two weeks at a time. I cried the day I finally had to put her in a nursing home. She lasted there only sixteen days.

She was my first sponsor—tough as nails, but also exquisitely gentle. At two-and-a-half years sober, I took a thorough Fifth Step with her. When I finished, she looked at me, smiled, and said, "Baby, you weren't all that good at being all that bad." This from a white-haired woman not quite five feet tall, who at one point had tested me on what length I would go to stay sober.

Our letters to one another are gems. I have them still. I have a whole book of important "sayings" from Ruby Ann's letters to me, and I read it periodically for inspiration. Even in the end, the pain from her cancer made her say, "Pain makes you bitter or better, and which depends upon your closeness to God."

The day when she took her last breath, I lit a jasmine candle next to her bed and was holding her hand, singing "Nearer My God to Thee" over and over, tears running. Built into all those emotions was the heightening love she brought to me, for individuals and for mankind.

Finally, she said, "We just flat don't realize how extremely fortunate we are! We got to AA before we had completely destroyed our adaptability—whew—close call for many of us. My God, my God, how blessed we are!"

HELEN W.
Napa, California

CHAPTER SEVEN

SANCTUARY

Recovery, with the help of sponsors both inside and outside the prison walls

"Individuals and groups should not and cannot afford to lose sight of the importance of sponsorship, the importance of taking special interest in a penalized alcoholic who wants to stop drinking and gain mental sobriety," writes an incarcerated AA in "An Inmate Member Gives Some Valuable Do's and Don'ts." "Sponsorship by an older member can mean much to a person in a prison."

For some, it was the work they did with their sponsors before going to jail that made the difference. "I was five months sober and working on Step Nine when I found out I was probably going to prison," the author of "Someone to Help" recounts. "My sponsor told me, 'Maybe there is someone God needs you to help in prison.' ... I don't know if I've found the person God wants me to help, but with everyone I meet I share my experience, strength and hope."

The stories in this chapter are about finding a sponsor in prison or being a sponsor to someone on the inside. Read about how this particular kind of AA experience helped them recover.

Someone to Help

July 2009

It seemed no matter what I did to quit drinking, it didn't work. I had been sober before, I had gone through the Steps, rehabs, jails, meetings. Then I asked someone to sponsor me. I knew that working the Steps would come after he said yes, if he did say yes.

God had the perfect sponsor for me; I just hadn't asked him yet. My sponsor said AA isn't for the people who need it or for the people who want it; it's for the people who are willing to do the work to get it. He said, "If you are willing to do the work that is required to work through the Steps and go to meetings and get a home group, I'll sponsor you." I really didn't believe going through the Steps with a sponsor would change my life and perspective, or light a passion in me the way it did. He described the Big Book and the Steps in a simple way, like no one has ever done before. I was doing the best I had in years. I turned my life over to God.

But in a way, I'd heard it all before. It's just mind-boggling. First, he explained the reason why the Big Book was published: so that an alcoholic can get a power sufficient enough that he doesn't have to drink. That's pretty heavy for a guy who was homeless, attending meetings and couldn't stop drinking. But it hit me like a ton of bricks.

Secondly, he taught me to pass the miracle on. My sponsor took me through the Steps the way Dr. Bob took his sponsees through the Steps, one right after the other. Something unbelievable was happening to me. I was five months sober and working on Step Nine when I found out I was probably going to prison. At first my lawyer said, "Don't worry about a thing." Things change fast. My sponsor told me, "Maybe there is someone God needs you to help in prison."

I've been in prison for 10 months now, and I still have a passion for AA and the Steps of Alcoholics Anonymous. I don't know if I've found the person God wants me to help, but with everyone I meet I share my experience, strength and hope.

God willing, next December I'll see my AA friends on the outside. If I hadn't taken the Steps with my sponsor before I came to prison, there's no telling where my life would have gone.

DIRK S.
Perry, Florida

A Smile to Offer

July 2006

In 1997, I was sentenced to twelve to fifteen years in prison as a direct result of my drinking. The unmanageability in my life was horrifying. I was hopeless and beat down so low that I never thought my life could be different. I wanted change but didn't know what I needed.

I began drinking at the age of twelve. Alcohol filled a void inside me and gave me courage to fit in. Chaos and severe consequences dominated the years of my drinking career. It became normal to me. It was normal and familiar to end up in jails and institutions. It was normal to lie, cheat, and steal.

I lost my family and children, and used and abused my friends. I ended up on my death bed more times than I can count. I wanted desperately to die but something wouldn't let me go. Even after being in prison for four-and-a-half years, I was still not convinced that drinking was my problem. Eaten up with resentments, I thought all of this was the judge's fault!

Only after the disease of alcoholism struck someone I loved did I become willing to change my own life. That someone was my son, who nearly died in an automobile accident because he was drinking and driving. Finally, the light bulb went off in my head. My son was lying in a hospital somewhere and I was in prison, locked away and unavailable.

I started going to meetings at the unit. I noticed something about the sponsors who came in from the outside. They smiled and had a peacefulness about them that I only dreamed of having. I, too, wanted to smile a real smile and wanted to know peace. But I was scared to death. I'd show up at meetings, sit in a corner, and be quiet. I wanted to reach out, but my shame, guilt, and low self-esteem wouldn't allow it.

One of the sponsors reached out to me. She sat with me every time she came to meetings. She spent time talking to me after the meetings. I started feeling some trust. It had been so long since anyone who lived right wanted to spend time with me. I finally asked the big question: would she sponsor me? "I thought you'd never ask," she said. We worked Steps One through Three. I was willing to do whatever she suggested.

They moved me to another unit. Although still full of fear, I knew that AA was working in my life. I had admitted I couldn't drink successfully. I came to believe that something much more powerful than me could restore me to sanity. I had some hope. I decided to let God run my life. I found the rooms of AA in the new unit where I was housed. Only one sponsor came in from the outside, and she was occupied with other sponsees.

I was determined to complete the Steps. I worked on my Fourth Step—just me, God, and the Big Book. I wrote for months and months until I felt I was ready for Step Five. Although I still didn't have a sponsor, I had access to the counselors who work here. I asked one if she knew someone I could do my Fifth Step with. The counselor set me up with one of her friends, who just happened to be in AA. I had already decided there were a few things I would never tell her or anyone else. I didn't think anyone would understand. After telling her my deep, dark secrets, I planned on never seeing her again. I intended to tell her what wasn't so painful and keep the rest stuck inside me, unaware that it would continue to keep me sick. But my Higher Power had other plans. I put everything out on the table that day. We stayed in a little office for hours going over my stuff. It was the most wonderful experience I've ever had.

This woman I never intended to see again became my sponsor. She worked with me for two years, going through the Steps, taking me to outside meetings, to her home group, to AA workshops, and to conventions. Early on, she suggested that we sit in the front row at meetings, that I share at every meeting, that I go up to the women after meetings, shake their hands and introduce myself. It was hard to do what she suggested, but I did it and am so grateful for her today. I have made so many friends in AA who accept me and welcome me. They loved me until I was able to love myself.

I am grateful for all the sponsors I've had in AA. All have taken me to different levels. They taught me about real life and living. They were walking Big Books.

I have worked through most of my resentments. Today I don't blame the judge for my actions. Today I have hope and an awesome relationship with my Higher Power. I have earned a cosmetology license and work at a wonderful salon through a work-release program. Four years have been taken off my sentence.

Most of my family is back in my life today. When I go home on passes each month, my father tells me he loves me and opens his home to me. I blow on the breathalyzer here at the unit and it says 0.00. These are all miracles for someone who was a hopeless and homeless alcoholic.

Some days I didn't think I could do it—the pain was too great. Now I know that the pains were growing pains. Today, the two most important things in recovery for me are willingness and action.

I sponsor women on the unit and give back what's been given so freely to me. Today, I have a smile that I can offer other alcoholics.

JOAN H.
Raleigh, North Carolina

From the Inside Out (Excerpt)

July 2003

I was sentenced to one hundred years in a maximum security prison. Hopeless and desperate, I had no meaningful future ahead of me except to spend year after countless year watching life pass me by. I was supposed to have potential, a future, a career, a place in society. But my anxieties, resentments, and shortcomings always sabotaged me. Trying to fill the hole in my soul, I used many things, including alcohol, and it ultimately led to crime and incarceration. There was no way out for me, and no reason for me to try any longer, I thought. Then I was introduced to Alcoholics Anonymous in prison, and my life began to change from the inside out. What could a program of recovery offer me?

Immediately I felt the spirit of enthusiasm and fellowship in the rooms of AA. For me, the meetings were a sanctuary from the bleak prison environment. I knew that I just plain felt better in the meetings, and that kept me coming back. Jim, an AA volunteer, became my sponsor.

I was absorbed in the process of helping others when an opportunity for release came my way. I had spent almost eleven years incarcerated up to that point and had a quality of living that far surpassed that of any previous time in my life. Trying to live one day at a time according to spiritual principles; staying in close connection with the AA Fellowship; and maintaining a trusting relationship with God and my sponsor had cumulatively carried me through my incarceration, and now I had a second chance at freedom! I remember an AA speaker telling me that when God has work for you to do, the walls come down. My sponsor and AA taught me that when the system shuts a door in your face, God opens a window. Having personally been turned down for parole nine times had given me perspective about trying to minimize my expectations in order to maximize my acceptance and serenity.

On Good Friday, 2002, I was released. My sponsor was waiting for me in the parking lot. We had talked ahead of time about the importance of jumping into the program as soon as my feet hit the pavement. Only twenty minutes after walking out of that prison, there I was, making my first stop in society at the Alano Club, and after that at the Serenity Center (two AA clubhouses in the area). Afterward, my sponsor drove me to the recovery house where I now live. That evening, I attended the ABC Group, my first AA meeting as a free man. Two days later, I celebrated Easter Sunday at my sponsor's house with his family. There were no happier or more grateful people in Maryland that day than the two of us.

My two years in AA have taught me that sponsorship, the Steps, and service work are the core actions to maintain my sobriety. Someday, I hope to carry the legacy of love and service back into a prison—to give back what was so generously passed on to me.

J. K.
Baltimore, Maryland

My Sponsor Took It Easy

July 1973

I've never yet been to an AA meeting, but I'm still an AA member, because the "Twelve and Twelve" says all I need to do is say so. I am looking forward to attending when the judge allows my sponsors to take me. You guessed it—I'm in jail.

Before this happened, Don invited me to come to meetings several times or even to stop in for coffee at his office. But I was too busy, you understand. How could I waste time and gasoline running around the country to meetings, and save enough money to stay drunk for a week or ten days or more at a time? I had responsibilities!

Soon after Don's efforts, I came to trial for driving under the influence. On my way to court, I acquired another citation for the same thing. Phil contacted me in jail, and though he had me cornered, he didn't press. My belligerent personality would have revolted. It is sometimes problem enough to lead the mule to water, much less suggest that he should drink—or not drink.

Phil brought the AA literature I needed—the Big Book, *Twelve Steps and Twelve Traditions*, past issues of the Grapevine, and the rest—and then seemed to take it for granted that I surely had enough gray matter left to glean something from them. He also brought a few other things I needed, and was always willing to talk when and if I was. Of course, all this wasn't easy for him. But he gave me no lectures and made no request for an immediate decision. He knew I needed time to understand that my supreme problem-solving ability did not always work.

Easy Does It has done it for me so far. At least, I swallowed some little facts. The real test will come when friends and a jug are before me, but I have some roots for abstinence already sprouting—my faith in AA and, above all, in a Higher Power, which to me is One who causes all things to work together for good to those who love God.

These words of infinite wisdom are meant to imply, not that a Johnny-come-lately knows a fraction of the things experience has taught the old-timers, but only that we are all different and some of us may stomp our feet, turn blue, and balk if we suspect we are being led to make any commitment. Being like a mule is not proper or reasonable, but it is one of the unenviable traits that helped me become an alcoholic.

C. B.
Waldport, Oregon

An Inmate Member Gives Some Valuable Do's and Don'ts (Excerpt)

May 1961

Most members of Alcoholics Anonymous owe their sobriety to the fact that someone else took a special interest in them and was willing to share a great gift with them. Sponsorship by an older member can mean much to a person in a prison, especially to the newcomer who turns to AA for help.

Individuals and groups should not and cannot afford to lose sight of the importance of sponsorship, the importance of taking special interest in a penalized alcoholic who wants to stop drinking and gain mental sobriety.

Those who will accept and do sponsorship work can and will be welcomed by the confined alcoholic, and such work helps the AA, himself, to grow. It also creates and deepens the satisfaction derived from helping others in an inspiring activity.

The outsider who asks himself the question "What does a sponsor do?" need only remember what AA did for him. The inmate hopes for a sincere sponsor, one who really wants to help and can serve as a concrete example. He wants encouragement, both written and verbal. He wants to be fully convinced and must be reminded to keep an open mind. Remember the sponsor you had, and all he said?

The experience of individual sponsors and groups has demonstrated conclusively that those who get the most out of the AA program, and do the most effective job of carrying the AA message to imprisoned alcoholics, are those to whom AA responsibilities are too important to be left to chance. Such members and groups welcome sponsorship and look upon it as an opportunity to enrich their own lives as well as those of the inmates they serve.

D. M.
Atlanta, Georgia

Six Days and Counting

July 2002

I have six days till I am released into a new style of living. When I first got here, my spiritual life was drained. I was on my last legs due to my drinking. After my system had been ridding itself of all the poisons I fed it for a month, I started to think clearly again. I told myself there are two ways that I could do this. I could sit in my cell and feel sorry for myself, or I could try to change.

The first thing I did was to find an AA sponsor. I wrote to the General Service Office and asked for assistance in finding one (the address is in the Big Book). Not knowing what to expect, I received a letter from the office that said I would be hearing from a prospective sponsor soon. Lo and behold, I did! This in itself astonished me and lifted my spirits. In the first letter that I wrote to my new sponsor, I asked him how I could live life again alcohol-free? To me this seemed impossible. I thought I could never do it. But my sponsor told me of this new way of living that he had found through AA, and he said he would pass it on to me. For the next fifteen months, it seemed to get easier for me to live with myself every day.

My new sponsor sent me the Grapevine as a gift, which has been a great inspiration to me. With it in my cell, I could open a meeting anytime with myself.

On the days that life seemed grim, I learned to pray to my Higher Power, and asked him to help me through the day. I've come to understand the Big Book, and that I'm not alone. I'm learning through working the Steps and "keeping it simple," that I too can get through it a day at a time.

What I really learned is that AA has plenty of tools to offer, but

I can't be afraid to get my hands dirty. I'm really looking forward to my first AA meeting on the outside. I know that this new way of living is a life-saver. Now I can leave here on both legs, but I will take baby steps.

GARY W.
Albion, Pennsylvania

CHAPTER EIGHT

NOTHING IN COMMON?

Old/young, gay/straight—unlikely pairs bond as sponsor and sponsee

"Ya know, Jim, I've been in jail ... I ain't got much education," says the young AA with experience to the older man—the newcomer—with several academic degrees, in the story "El Garage." The educated newcomer isn't sure it will work, but he and this unlikely sponsor find common ground.

In "Finding the Very Best Sponsor in AA," a 21-year-old member abandons his "laundry list of qualities" for a sponsor when a 68-year-old AA veteran helps him find much-needed serenity. "For the first time in my life, someone else was able to calm that perfect storm between my ears," he writes.

There was no explanation for it; these members simply found sponsors they could identify with and trust. In the next few pages, read how it's the message, not the messenger, that counts in passing on the program of recovery.

El Garage

May 1991

The first time I admitted out loud that I was an alcoholic I was in a little twenty-four-hour group down a back street in Mexico City. When I moved back to the States I went to my first U.S. meeting at an Alano Club. I got there half an hour early and circled the block so as not to spend more time inside than I had to. I didn't like the meeting. It was a blue-collar, tattooed crowd, with not very elegant language and too much smoke. So I looked in the AA directory of another county, close by and well-to-do. For three months I drove to a Sunday night open meeting. It was in a bank, not far from a university. Here, I thought, I would find a somewhat better vocabulary and a Ph.D. for a sponsor, as my education, profession, and cultural level deserved. After all, I was both a priest and a psychologist.

Then a young guy at that meeting told me about a Monday night men's stag meeting. He promised that they wouldn't sit me in the middle of a circle and beat me to death with "tough love," whatever that might be. He said they would be nice and they were. But I still didn't open up at either group. Out of shame, fear, and false pride, I just showed up and sat there. I did relate to the young fellow who had reached out his hand when I first arrived. Any problems or questions I had I saved for him.

After three months it occurred to me that I wasn't getting anywhere. I saw all kinds of people laughing and kidding and taking walks with their sponsors. And they seemed to like each other, even hugging in a way which seemed sincere, natural, and relaxed. I was impressed and attracted but didn't know how to get into whatever it was they had. One night I was hurting and lonely, alone in the crowd. I was wiping the tables after the meeting and no one offered to help me. The crowd was thinning out and going home or to a coffee shop for the "meeting after the meeting," and I was being left alone. I thought, Is it possible to come here lonely and go home lonelier than ever? Poor me! At that point a voice came from over by the door. It was Cristobal, called Chris, a young guy, dark, with a big black mustache and a way of sharing that was deep, sincere, and showed a very sensitive nature.

The next week I made sure I sat next to him during the closing prayer. When we joined hands I could feel that his were calloused. I thought to myself, You came looking for a Ph.D. and are going to wind up with a wheelbarrow pusher. Chris helped me in his own mysterious way—simple, direct, effective.

I now had five months going to meetings, "on" the program much more than "in" it, and I was desperate. Flat on my back and at last reaching a hand up for help, I was hardly in a position to ask for credentials. I asked Chris to be my sponsor.

He said, "I'll give you my phone number, Jim, and you think about it for twenty-four hours. If you still want to, give me a call, and I'll tell you how to get to my house."

I found his house, an alley with little working-class houses on each side. His was the last house on the biggest lot. His old car was up on blocks, his license not suspended but revoked for three years. He introduced me to his wife and two little kids (one more on the way), and brought me to a place I've gotten more and more familiar with over the years—his garage, or "Ga-RA-hey," as we say it in Spanish. The garage was cluttered with camping gear, car parts, bicycles, and what not. There was a beat-up old TV and a reclining chair that Chris's sponsor had given him. Next to it was a shelf with the Big Book, the "Twelve and Twelve," *As Bill Sees It*, *Twenty-Four Hours a Day*, and pads "for when I do my writing."

Chris sat me down on the reclining chair, sat himself into a lawn chair, put his feet on the TV, and started off: "Ya know, Jim, I've been in jail." It turned out that he had been in a jail where I had been chaplain many years before. Then, giving me a quick glance out of the corner of his eye: "I ain't got much education. They kicked me out of high school with a diploma just to get rid of me 'cause I was raising so much fuss. I suppose you gotta lot of degrees." I owned up to having a few, sort of casually specifying that some of them were on the graduate level. He turned those dark eyes on me and turned to the matter of religion. "I ain't got no religion. I went to my wife's church to get married, ain't been back since, and don't intend to." I replied that I wasn't looking for a spiritual director, but a sponsor. (I didn't realize at the time that they are pretty much the same thing. A sponsor is one who teaches me to walk with God according to the Twelve Steps.) Then, looking squarely at me, he said, "Do you still want me to be your sponsor?" Because of his openness and honesty, and *manera de ser* or "way of being," I was now more convinced than ever. "Yes," I replied. And then something started which hasn't ended.

Chris leaned back in his chair, settled his feet comfortably on the TV and said, "Tell me, Jim, about your drinking." He had a way about him that kept drawing me out. If I stumbled or faltered out of shame or pain, he would throw something of his own in which was worse than mine. I thought, It is pretty hard to win at can-you-top-this around here. There was such compassion in his eyes and voice that he kept me going. After a while he couldn't slow me down. There had been so much piled up inside me for so long, that once started it had to come out. Most of the time I was looking down out of shame. When I would take a quick glance up to see if it was still safe, all I saw was that at last I had found the person and the moment. I kept going. Things came out that I didn't know were there, things which nothing, even professional counseling, had ever brought to light. When at last I was finished I was looking down at the oil-stained cement floor and crying softly. Chris waited a while and then said, "What do you feel, Jim?" I stopped crying and coughed up from somewhere deep inside of me, "I feel very sorry and very ashamed."

And he walked out.

With all that junk piled up in the garage, I couldn't see where he had gone. It had been daylight when I started speaking, but I could see that it was dark outside now and the stars were shining. I know what priests do and what shrinks do, but sponsors are something else, I thought. They get all the worst out of you and then walk away. Then the by-now familiar voice came floating in, "Come on out here, Jim." And I came out. I was twice his age and yet I was obeying him like a little kid. I didn't have much choice. My way hadn't worked and he was offering me a way out.

When I got outside, I found him standing, feet apart, hands behind his back, looking into the stars. "I got a friend up there, Jim, and I kinda check things out with him to make sure they are okay so stuff won't hit the fan and land on me. But my friend says it's okay. Come over here, Jim." Once more I did what I was told. When I came over, he just hugged me and let me cry on his shoulder. For thirty years as a priest and fifteen as a psychologist, others had cried on my shoulder. Now it was my turn. "Get it all out, Jim." The longer and deeper I cried, the harder he hugged me. Finally I stopped.

"Is that all of it, Jim?" "Chris, for now that's all I have." Somehow or other, even then, I had the intuition that more would be revealed.

Somewhat embarrassed, I was looking down. "Look up, Jim." I looked up, a little. "Look me in the eye, Jim." I looked him in the eye. He held me at arm's length, one hand on each shoulder. He looked into me for a while, nodded his head in approval, and said the words which were to become my turning point, my new pair of glasses, my moment of truth—whatever you want to call it. Looking deep inside me he said, "Jim, it's all right to be human." Then he sort of slapped me on the right side of my face, wiping the tears away, and sent me into the house to wash up, for "we're going to a meeting."

A few days later, I went to my clergy group and told them of my experience, summing it up by dramatically stating, "So that unchurched pagan heard the best confession I ever made." They laughed and one old-timer with an Irish brogue and a twinkle in his eye said, "So who is the 'pagan' now?"

That was chapter one in an ongoing series which might be called, "My Sponsor and I." Chris is coming up on five years now and I'm coming up on three. I wouldn't miss those sessions in *el garage* for anything. Somehow, I suspect, neither would Chris.

ANONYMOUS

Finding the Very Best Sponsor in AA

October 2008

When I first got sober a few years ago, old-timers stressed how important it was to get a sponsor, and I created a laundry list of qualities I wanted in the "perfect sponsor." Unfortunately, no one matched that list. I was twenty-one and had quite a few drugs in my story, as well as myriad other idiosyncrasies I thought were unique to me. I decided that my sponsor would have to be young, would have to understand my lingo, and at least would have experimented with drugs.

After a few tries at sobriety, a lot of coffee, quite a few meetings, and one really big cross-country move, all within less than a month of getting sober, I found John. He wasn't someone who met my criteria. My laundry list, like so many other ideas I had then, was quickly overturned. What I did find was the best sponsor in AA. John, a young sixty-eight years old, shook his head and smiled as I scribbled his number down on a piece of cardboard ripped from my pack of cigarettes. The next day we had a cup of coffee together. After a number of rides to meetings in his big old '89 Lincoln—which I ridiculed—I finally worked up the intestinal fortitude to ask him to sponsor me.

During the next few months, I relished the many hours I spent in the front seat of that Lincoln. I hung on to John's every word. Okay, not every word, but most words. For the first time in my life, someone else was able to calm that perfect storm between my ears.

I listened nostalgically to stories of a time in AA I had never known, a time of even bigger cars and smoke-drenched Twelfth Step calls under the cover of night. I'm still enthralled by John's stories, no matter how many times I've heard them. Besides, there is always an occasional new one in the mix.

John never had to tell me to call him every day, because I wanted to call him every day. When John wasn't home, his wife Sharon was a superb backup with her thirty-plus years of sobriety. I've never felt as safe as I did sitting in that living room with their years of sobriety surrounding me. I joked to other old-timers about the Christmas lights John "forced" me to hang and the boxes he "forced" me to lift in order to stay sober. They would laugh and say, "Well, you didn't drink, did you? He must be doing something right."

I now live some distance away from John, but some of my favorite times continue to be at his dining room table. He still doesn't understand my loud rap music, but he knows me.

I do have the best sponsor in AA, but there are thousands of "best sponsors" around us at every meeting. All it takes is some open-mindedness and willingness. Much to my surprise, I didn't have to conduct extensive interviews to find mine; just a cup of coffee and an invitation of friendship were enough.

For me that's what sponsorship truly is: friendship. John was not a name I could use to appease the powers that be, and I was not just someone he could claim as another "pigeon." I was a friend—a best friend with whom he could share the beauty of what he had found in Alcoholics Anonymous.

PATRICK C.
Oakland, California

Not My Choice

November 2007

I didn't pick my sponsor and I didn't particularly like her when I met her. But I was in treatment, again, and when I was preparing to leave, the treatment team asked me if I had a sponsor. I said no—but I'd be sure to get one once I got out.

Knowing that that was probably not going to happen, the treatment team assigned me a temporary sponsor. I was set to meet her at an Alcoholics Anonymous meeting the day I was discharged. Amazingly enough, I followed through and met Kathy S. for the first time at a clubhouse in Tallahassee, Florida, on November 3, 1990. As soon as I saw her, I knew we had nothing in common.

She was a fifth-grade schoolteacher. I was a biker babe. She wore colorful clothes with matching accessories. I always wore black and my accessories were chains and a switchblade. She rarely cursed. It was six months before I learned to use the word "mother" by itself. She had her life together and mine was spiraling out of control. I did not listen to what she said, and I did not stay sober.

With her help and guidance, I went back to treatment in January 1991. Since that day, I have not found it necessary or worthwhile to take a drink. I learned a lot in treatment and decided to put the suggestions I had been given into practice.

Although I was stark raving mad, Kathy was willing to work with me. In time, I began to trust her. In all of the years we have worked together, she has never led me astray. I have never been asked to do anything detrimental or bad for me as a recovering alcoholic and human being.

She taught me about "the box" in life. "The box" was empty and had nothing inside. Kathy said I was settling for it. She told me that I deserved all the pretty tissue paper in different colors, the brilliant wrapping paper, and the luxurious bows—and the gifts that could come inside the box.

She taught me that gifts are not necessarily material goods. Sometimes, gifts couldn't be seen, only felt. For instance: The gift of a good night's sleep, the gifts of integrity, self-respect, and the ability to value myself as a human being. My sponsor taught me that I deserved to recover and I was worthy of all the gifts that sobriety had to offer. But these things didn't happen overnight. Just like the Promises in the Big Book, I had to work for them.

I made a lot of meetings, I worked the Steps, I found a Higher Power, I made amends, and I tried to help others. Somewhere along the line, I began to find myself. I exchanged my colorful language for colorful clothes. I found the gifts of laughter, friendship, and peace of mind. The woman who was once cloaked in black was left behind.

My sponsor saw each triumph. She watched me while I went back to college and earned a degree. She was by my side when I was granted a full pardon from the governor of Florida for the things I had done—the wreckage of my past.

My sponsor also was present during my times of grief and pain. When my son was arrested, shortly before Christmas 1997, I was devastated. What kind of gift was that—and right before Christmas? But Kathy showed me the gift I'd received: I found I could handle myself with dignity and grace, something I had known nothing about before. And I didn't have to drink over it.

My sponsor also taught me to accept life on life's terms, that the universe did not revolve around me. (Sometimes, I still argue with that one!) She told me to accept responsibility for my behavior.

It's been a few twenty-four hours since Kathy and I first met. We have been through a lot together and I know that without her wonderful wisdom and gentle touch, I wouldn't be the woman I am today.

I've since moved to another state and I don't see her much. I've traded Harleys for horses and my switchblade for a hoof pick. But I will never trade my time with Kathy. She is always with me, wherever I go.

SUSAN K.
Asheville, North Carolina

Good Friends

February 1989

Nine years ago, when I had just a few years of sobriety, I met a young man at an open meeting. We chatted a while and then Matthew (which is not his real name) took a seat next to mine as the meeting began. When it was over, we exchanged pleasantries and comments about interesting parts of the speaker's story. Soon I said goodbye and left to drive home since I live twenty miles from our meeting place and was even then an older lady.

There was something about this young man that made me uneasy. I wasn't sure what it was but it troubled me. I'd been in the program long enough to know that we are people from all walks of life, with many kinds of backgrounds, and none of us come into AA when our lives are going well. Matthew said he'd come in from the street and not with the help of a detoxification center. I'd heard prison stories and I wondered if something like that could have accounted for the strange, anxious look in his eyes.

The next week, having forgotten all about Matthew, I happily headed for my weekly open meeting. Just as I found a seat, who should greet me, asking politely if he could sit beside me, but Matthew. I was glad to see him and, as before, we talked together as the crowd assembled.

I was rather pleased with Matthew's attention since he was the age of my youngest child, a son for whom I was quite lonesome at the time. However, after several more weeks of the same behavior, my friend seemed to be overdoing things. I even wondered if this young man had some kind of crush on me. Oh my goodness, I thought, if true, what will I do about that?

The next week, when Matthew sat down in the chair beside me, I said softly, yet firmly and directly into his ear, "Young man, I don't have any designs upon you." His face turned quickly toward mine and he stammered, "Oh no, I didn't mean anything like that. I have just been trying to ask you to be my sponsor."

I knew it was not advisable for a woman to sponsor a man and I said so. I recommended he ask a man and his disappointment was apparent. I was sorry.

In the meantime I asked Tom, an old-timer, what I could do about all this. Rubbing his chin thoughtfully, he said, "Tell him you will sponsor him by phone only." This I did and as I expected, Matthew was very pleased. He phoned me regularly and we became quite well acquainted. He worked his program diligently. But there was still that look in his eye. Had he done some terrible thing? Perhaps even killed somebody? I didn't know. Something was bothering him deeply.

Winter passed into spring, and in late summer Matthew asked if he could bring his mother to meet me. They would come, by appointment, to my place of business and not to my home. I felt that would be okay. They came and I was impressed. His mother was lovely. She was about my age and we had much in common. Our visit was most enjoyable.

October arrived again and Matthew had been sober almost a year. One day he called to ask—urgently—if he could talk with me personally. He hoped he could come right away. I consented.

I live alone and was still somewhat wary. It would take Matthew about half an hour to get there. We could meet in the park, for it was a beautiful warm day and there would be lots of people there. I suggested this and Matthew was pleased to accept.

I drove my small white camper to the park and arranged two folding chairs outside. This would be a good place for us to talk and there were many people nearby enjoying this autumn day. When Matthew drove in, I waved to him. It was good to see him and for the first time we hugged each other. Sitting in the chairs outside the camper, our conversation was enjoyable. I wondered what serious subject Matthew had come to discuss. Perhaps coffee would make our meeting seem like a real one. I bravely invited Matthew into the camper while I made the coffee, and we sat at the small table, continuing to talk.

Suddenly Matthew, leaning forward, looked directly into my eyes and said, "There is something I have to tell you. I am gay."

Yes, I was surprised. But relief flooded over me as I shook my head saying, "Is that all that's the matter? I thought you had killed somebody!" He quietly said, "No," as tears welled in his eyes. The strange, anxious look, now so familiar to me, actually faded as he spoke. We laughed and we cried together. The truth had been told and it was all right.

Eight years have passed since that October day. Matthew and I call each other frequently and go places together occasionally. We are good friends.

M. V.
Elk Rapids, Michigan

That's My Sponsor!

June 1978

Mark Twain said something to this effect: "When I was sixteen, I couldn't believe how stupid my father was. By the time I was twenty-one, it was amazing how much the old man had learned!"

That aptly expresses the way I felt about my sponsor. He seemed so "simple" when he twelfth-stepped me. I remember thinking, Sure, he's happy, but if I didn't drink and mess around, I'd miss everything that intelligent people love. I mean, after all, coffee sessions were great for planning the next drinking session, but did this large (six feet four, 230 pounds) individual mean to tell me that this was it? Coffee, a few laughs, then home, and that was living? That was sobriety? Next!

It took many coffee sessions, much talking, plenty of persistence, and a lot of laughter and tears before I even started to see that this simple life was in fact what I'd been searching for. I heard a difference in the laughter. It was from the gut and not from the bottle. I remember the phone ringing and that man telling me that I was a liar and a phony. Sometimes, I would say, "If you don't have anything nice to say ..." etc., and then there would be the sound of silence.

Finally, he sensed that I had reached the saturation point, and he didn't call for two weeks. I began to miss him. But I recall telling my wife at one point that if that gigantic Norwegian lout ever set foot in my house again, I would call the police. (After all, he was too big to throw out. Besides, who would have the guts to try that sober?) It was good I had heard early in AA that people who change sponsors frequently are trying to control the environment rather than change themselves. I must admit the thought of getting a new sponsor did occur to me, in my somewhat deflated brain.

Instead, strangely enough, I began to tell people in AA with a great deal of pride that he was my sponsor.

What a change!

Then, when all seemed well—I had "pigeons" of my own, a better quality of sobriety, and more friends than I had ever had in my life—the bottom seemingly fell out. This man (note—no longer a lout) announced that he and his family were departing the scene. They were moving, and it wasn't across the street.

I waited. No self-pity, no anger, no jealousy, no hate. What had this program done to me? I tried desperately to regain some of the old style. Perhaps just a snit or a few well-chosen cusswords? No, all I could produce was a genuine feeling of love for him and his family, and a wish for their well-being.

I believe today that although he worked through my problems with me, he made sure that they remained my problems. To him and to Alcoholics Anonymous, I will remain eternally grateful. And wherever sponsors like this man are found, there will be a high standard of sobriety and many gratefully deflated drunks.

M.J.
Saskatoon, Saskatchewan

CHAPTER NINE

START EACH DAY WITH A MIRACLE

These desperate alcoholics never thought AA would work for them. But working with their sponsors, they broke through and started to recover.

A man who is facing the reality that he abandoned his kids in "No Quick Fix"; a woman dealing with the baggage of an abusive ex in "A Matter of Choice"; and the other "tough cases" in this chapter find the love and guidance they need to get through their pain. "My sponsor told me to start each day with a miracle," the author of "Joanie's God" writes. "1. I woke up; I didn't come to. 2. I had a roof over my head and food in my belly. 3. I could see, touch, smell, hear and taste. And then I was to look for 'coincidences' throughout my day. These could be called miracles, usually. I did this every day and, incredibly, I began to be grateful and trust God a little bit." The stories in this chapter are by AAs who got and stayed sober no matter what life handed them—with the help of their sponsors.

No Quick Fix

September 2007

I was around AA for about fifteen years before I got into it. For a long time, I believed AA was a great program. It seemed to work for a lot of people; it just wouldn't work for me.

This time, for whatever reason, I finally came to the conclusion that I would never be able to stop drinking, and I had nowhere else to turn—except AA. I started attending meetings and I joined a group. I got a sponsor. But, for some reason, when I got together with him, we would talk about everything in the world except what was going on inside of me. I would be dying inside, and I would ask, "What are you up to this weekend?" or "What did you think of that car that drove by?"

Meanwhile, after the meetings I found myself sitting with this other guy, John. He would ask how I was, and for some reason I would tell him. I eventually asked him to be my sponsor. He was about five years sober and had a lot of time to talk to me.

Over the following few weeks, we got together every day. We went to the park, sat in my apartment or in the coffee shop, and we would talk. I told him everything. At least I thought I told him everything.

At least once a week, we would get together with another friend to study the Big Book and the Steps. Sometimes, other guys would come over as well, and we would listen to speaker tapes and read and talk about the program.

We became friends, and I started going over to John's house from time to time to visit and watch movies. One evening, we were watching a movie in his living room about recovery from alcoholism.

John had two sons and a daughter. His little girl was about the same age as the daughter I had abandoned some five years before. I watched as this beautiful little girl walked across the room, climbed up into John's lap, put her head on his chest, looked up into his face, and said, "I love you, Daddy."

I cannot put into words the pain I felt at that moment. I had a hole inside me and a fear worse than anything I had ever felt before. I panicked. I told John that the movie was "triggering me," and I left. I went home and cried and tried to keep from killing myself. I had told John about all the things I had done in the past that I couldn't change, but I had never talked about stuff that was going on in the present.

Again, I had no choice. The only way I knew how to deal with anything was to either get drunk or to tell someone. I went back to John's house and, after a little while, I finally told him why I left the previous day. I told him about the two kids I had abandoned, and how empty and scared and alone I felt.

He didn't have any magic advice for me. He had no quick fix or cure for my pain, and he didn't pretend that it was "okay." What he did do was hold me close while I cried. And he said the most important thing I have ever heard. He said, "Joe, we're going to get through this together."

Immediately, I felt it. I was not alone anymore. I have trouble describing the feeling I had. It was absolute faith that I was not alone in the world. I knew we would get through it. And one day at a time, we did.

My group had *we will get through this together* printed on my one-year medallion. A few months later, I followed some direction and found out where my children were. I went to my ex-wife, and she allowed me to start seeing my kids again.

Not long after that, I was sitting in my living room one Saturday evening. I watched as the most beautiful little girl I had ever seen walked across the room, climbed up into my lap, put her head on my chest, looked into my eyes, and said, "I love you, Daddy." I cried again. Again, I felt one of the most intense feelings I have ever had. It was a feeling of complete love, the ability to give and receive, and the knowledge that, without a doubt, I am not alone anymore.

I celebrated three years of sobriety this last December. I have my kids every other weekend, holidays, and every other chance I get to see them. My family is back in my life, and I know today that no matter what happens, we will get through it together.

It was made possible by the grace of God, the program in the book *Alcoholics Anonymous*, and a sponsor who knew enough not to try to fix something he could not. He knew enough to be there, hold me, love me, and share the love and experience that was given to him. The only way I know how to try to pay back this debt is to share my story and to do my best to share the love that was given to me.

JOE D.
Stratford, Ontario

Joanie's God (Excerpt)

August 2009

Before I came into Alcoholics Anonymous, I had closed the door on any belief I had ever had in a God. I blamed him for whatever had happened to me. When I was 11 years old, one morning before I left for school I asked my sweet mother for a quarter. She told me "not today," so I took it from her purse. That afternoon, a priest came to school and told me my mother had died. I knew it was my punishment for taking the quarter that morning! I threw the quarter down a street drain and said, "There, God—I gave it back! I won't spend it. Now bring my mother back!" No answer.

That was the beginning of a life believing that whenever anything bad happened to me, it was God punishing me.

On July 9, 1983, I said three magic words: "God help me." I believe in that one moment I was reaching out to the God I was told about way back at age 6. He responded, because the next day I crawled into the rooms of Alcoholics Anonymous—helpless, hopeless and unemployable. I knew what I had to do. I looked for women at all the meetings I went to—and there were many—and asked one to be my sponsor. She asked me whether I believed in God, and I answered, "Yes; in case there is one." She said, "Use mine; he does good work!" So every morning I got on my knees and said, "Dear Joanie's God: You know I don't mean what I'm saying. I'm only doing it because I was told to do it." And then I would ask Joanie's God to keep me away from a drink that day. And I thanked Joanie's God every night. That first sponsor talked to me in slogans, and it drove me crazy, but it worked for me till I got the fuzziness out of my head. At three months sober I got another sponsor who guided me through the Steps.

And I didn't drink! So I kept praying to Joanie's God. I didn't want to remind the God I had that I was around or where I was (as though he didn't know).

My sponsor told me to start each day with a miracle: 1. I woke up; I didn't come to. 2. I had a roof over my head and food in my belly. 3. I could see, touch, smell, hear and taste. And then I was to look for "coincidences" throughout my day. These could be called miracles, usually. I did this every day and, incredibly, I began to be grateful and trust God a little bit.

Many years later, I still do the same things I did during my first years of sobriety. I don't tell God what to do. If I did, I would be playing God and he does such wonderful work I don't want to louse it up.

JEANNE R.
Monaca, Pennsylvania

Get a Cat

July 2003

My sponsor was one of those sponsors who intuitively know "how to handle situations which used to baffle us." I remember when I was a few weeks sober, I told my sponsor I was lonely. He told me to get a cat. I told him I wasn't interested in cats. He said he didn't care and that I should get a cat. Well, what did he know? I had been doing quite a bit of chatting on the computer, and I had met this girl. She lived in Wyoming. She told me she loved me. I was forty years old, and I couldn't remember the last time someone had told me that. So, I did the only thing I could think of. I quit my job and moved to Wyoming.

My sponsor said it was a geographical cure and that I would be much better off if I just got a cat. I told him that he was wrong, that there was no cure. I told him I knew I was powerless over alcohol. I told him it didn't make any difference if I was in Halifax or Wyoming, I would still go to meetings and I would still be sober. He made some remark about a cat.

When I was on a train leaving Nova Scotia, the waiter went past with his little cart of goodies. I noticed a tall boy of Keith's ale, my favorite beer. Suddenly, the thought occurred to me, I bet they don't make Keith's in Wyoming. I should have one for the road to celebrate my new beginning.

Well, this is where rational thinking departed and the insanity of the first drink took over—the insanity that I could think for a second that, under any circumstances, I could have one of anything. Three weeks later, I was hitchhiking through a snowstorm on the Trans Canada Highway with five pieces of luggage, looking for an AA meeting.

My sponsor had been speaking to me in what I have come to

know as Newcomer Language. He said simple things. Some were slogans like "Keep It Simple" and "First Things First." Some were quotes from AA literature, like the Promises and the "musts." Others were just things he made up—for example, "Get a cat." He could have said, "The primary fact we fail to recognize is our total inability to form a true partnership with another human being." "We have not once sought to be one in a family, to be a friend among friends, to be a worker among workers, to be a useful member of society. ... This self-centered behavior blocked a partnership relation with any one of those about us. Of true brotherhood we had small comprehension."

He might have said all that, and maybe he did. Maybe he knew I wouldn't understand all that. So, he just said, "Get a cat." It's like when he used to say, "Make coffee" or "Sit up front and be quiet" or "There always looks better than here until you get there."

Needless to say, I did find that AA meeting. When the meeting was over, I got in touch with my sponsor and told him I was ready to listen now. I have been listening, too. I have done whatever he suggested no matter whether or not I understood it at the time. That was five years ago. Today, I have a new freedom and a new happiness. I have a wife. I have a family. I have a job. And yes, I finally did get a cat.

BERNIE S.
Dartmouth, Nova Scotia

A Matter of Choice

September 2005

I am so grateful for sponsorship in the program of Alcoholics Anonymous. Without it, I would never have made it.

Women sponsors have taught me how to live life on life's terms. There have been many times during my thirteen-year sober journey when I have gone on the faith that my sponsor had. When I don't see the way through the fog, and when it just seems too hard, God works through others to let me know that it's okay to move to the next step.

I am a single parent of three children, ages eight, ten, and twelve. I moved back to California after living in Colorado for two years. The move to Colorado was a last-ditch effort to make a disastrous relationship work; you know, I always have one more great idea ...

I had met this man in the throes of alcoholism and drug addiction. We were really just a couple of kids suffering from this disease, and we didn't even know it. He attempted to throw me out of a moving car on our first date, but that wasn't enough evidence for me to never go out with him again.

While drinking, the abuse was much worse: he fractured my ribs while I was pregnant, held me hostage in a motel room, and one time he choked me until I passed out. When I got sober, he decided to quit using and drinking as well, only he did it on his own, without any program. This, as we know in AA, is called dry drunkenness, and it was worse for the family than if he had simply drunk.

But I continued, by the grace of God, to seek help and to try to clear up the wreckage of my past. I was afraid to leave; he had threatened me long ago, saying that if I tried he would hunt me down like a dog and kill me. I believed him. Probably a lot of fear about raising my children alone helped me to stay, even though I was already doing everything on my own.

After one final physical attack, I took my children and left while their father was still in jail. We came to California, driving a moving van full of pots, pans, and whatever else I could throw in it. I was a wreck. The kids were wrecks. I hadn't slept with both eyes closed in about a year, and I had constant bladder infections, ulcers—every stress-related disorder you could imagine.

I cried out to God for help, and he started to put teachers into my life. I met my first sponsor in a women's meeting in Fullerton. She helped me to find new ways to support my family using the Seventh Tradition—which states that the AA groups themselves ought to be fully supported by the voluntary contributions of their own members—as a way to live my own life. She promised me that I would begin to feel better as soon as I worked at being less dependent on others both financially and emotionally.

So I started taking classes, first to become a nurse's aide and then a medical assistant. The kids and I slept on the floor of my mother's studio apartment in Brea, so I was fortunate not to have to pay rent. Unfortunately, this was not my attitude at that time! I have had to live with the fact that I complained and whined constantly in meetings about my misfortune. "Poor me," they would all say and then crack up into hysterics. This was all done to help me to get over my huge defect of self-pity, and it worked.

I worked at a gas station as a cashier to have money for food and other necessities. I spent a lot of time studying the Big Book behind that glass window. I learned so much from that job, how to suit up and show up, literally. One of the other problems I had was that I didn't like rules. The gas station uniform needed a little sprucing up, or so I thought. On every shift I would come in with it tied in the front or unbuttoned too low, anything to be different. This caused many unnecessary conflicts with my manager. People in the program said, "Just tuck the shirt in and be nice." So I did, and it worked!

The problem of not sleeping continued long after my arrival in California. Even the kids couldn't sleep. I would wake up in the middle of the night with the sensation of the barrel of a shotgun on my forehead, cold and smooth. Terror ran through my body. I would just shake and sob. I hit my knees in a desperate rendition of the Lord's Prayer, and even if it was in the middle of the night, I called my sponsor. She never yelled at me or treated me like a second-class citizen. In her quiet, relaxed voice she would ask, "What's up?" and I would open up my soul. By the end of the conversation she usually had me laughing so hard about some story from her life that I had forgotten what was wrong with me in the first place. When it was time to hang up, I would say, "Do you think I'll sleep tonight?" and she would say, "I will pray for you. Everything's going to be okay." That stuff is priceless. I believed her, and some time after that, the insomnia started to get better.

I learned the difference between a want and a need from sponsors in the program. My list of things I needed to buy with my paycheck had been something like this: $20 for the tanning booth, $15 for Starbucks, $10 to put gas in the car, $30 for the movies, $20 to take the kids to McDonald's—you know, all the essentials. So it was through much pain and humiliation that I learned to contribute to the rent by giving my mom some money each month, and I quit tanning after one Step study meeting when the subject was on the seven deadly sins. An old-timer said to me afterward, "Talk about vanity—look at that tan you have." I was so hurt, but it worked! Today, it's amazing how little I need to be happy. I think it's the gratitude for what I have that God has put in my heart that's changed me.

I shared constantly about what "he" had done to me, and all the things that "he" continued to do, like not pay child support and yelling at me on the phone. More lessons were to be learned. My sponsor suggested that I go to the district attorney to get child support, which was something that I had a lot of fear about. I'll never forget the feeling of opening the mailbox and seeing a check in it. As also suggested, I put a sign on the wall by the phone that I would be forced to see that said, "Hang up the phone!" When he started to scream or manipulate, I learned to just hang up. It worked!

I can remember one meeting in particular when I was full of self-pity and going on and on about "him" and an old-timer asked, "Well, who picked him, honey?" Well, that really fired me up; I thought to myself, I'll never share about him again! And so I learned to share about what "I" was doing, or, more importantly, not doing.

Then came the time when, after working as a medical assistant and learning how to use money a little more wisely, I got my own place. I really grew up; being the mother and the father, you learn really quickly what's important. I went to work and meetings, I met with my sponsor and did the laundry. I found true happiness and contentment in doing what God wanted me to do.

I had applied for HUD housing years earlier, and finally I got on the program, only the apartment building that we lived in didn't accept HUD funding. So I started to look for one that would and found that many landlords won't take it. My sponsor continued to have faith, even when I had none; she felt sure that I would find a place before the deadline was up. I can still hear her saying, "Sometimes, God waits until the very last hour, even minute, but he will answer." So I went on her faith, just like every other time when I thought things couldn't possibly work out.

The day before HUD was about to expire, I found our condo in Brea. To me, it's paradise. My sponsor used to tell me when I complained about living with my mom, "Fix up the place as much as you can, make it beautiful, and as soon as you really start to like it, it will be time to leave." So I learned how to make a comfortable, safe, and loving home for my family and me.

I have gone back to college in an attempt to support my family in a more appropriate way. I never thought this would be possible, but my sponsor kept on encouraging me. Once again, I went on her faith. It has been a struggle with financial insecurity. I don't see how we are getting by, but something always comes through. This semester, I was nominated for a journalism scholarship. Right away, I thought, No way will I get it. They don't know who I am. However, my professor called me this week to let me know that I got the scholarship and that the announcement dinner is this month. This is truly a victory that I owe to the program and, of course, to my God.

My Higher Power gives me wonderful gifts, and he likes to involve a lot of people in the process. Having faith is following through with my sponsor's suggestions even when it doesn't make sense.

I am learning to trust in God and in the program of Alcoholics Anonymous more and more every day, one day at a time.

KARA P.
Brea, California

You've Got to Give to Get (Excerpt)

June 2009

I was not prepared to do the Fourth Step, the moral inventory, and there was no way in heck that I was ever going to do the Fifth. I was never going to reveal my darkest secrets to anyone. They would go to the grave with me. I couldn't see how doing any of it would do me any good.

Not moving forward with the Steps left me only on the fringes of AA. I had always felt that the people there had the ability to see through me, that they could tell what I was thinking without my saying a word. That feeling inside started to get very uncomfortable. I stopped praying, and I cut down on meetings until I wasn't going at all. It did not take long for my insanity to return.

I didn't take a drink, but my depression and anxiety grew and grew. Every month or so, one friend from my home group would call. I had gotten to know him well in the short time I had been in the program. We often went fishing together after work. He was the most serene person I had ever met.

"How are you doing?" he would ask. "Fine," I would lie.

"Well, I just called to see how you were doing." And that was it. This went on for 10 months. The longer it went, the worse I felt, until finally I had enough. I was at last tormented enough to tell the truth and to reach out for help. I wasn't fine. I was awful. My life seemed to be crashing in around me and there was nothing I could do about it. He listened and cared.

I am eternally grateful to my friend. Today I believe that because he reached out my life was saved. With his help I had the courage (or humility) to return to meetings.

When I returned to AA I was able to find what I needed in the "John Wayne" group. We called it that because we did not hold hands during the Our Father. Everyone stood alone. We shook hands, but there wasn't any hugging. This isn't what everyone needs, but it worked for me at the time.

They were a bunch of crusty old-timers and they didn't take any of my crap. A guy with 10 years was still considered a kid in those meetings. I wanted to whimper and whine and complain, but they wouldn't let me get away with it. "We focus on the solution here, not the problem," they would say.

After nearly two years of white-knuckling it, I finally had the courage (or grace) to ask someone to be my sponsor. He was one of the toughest of the tough. I said, "You scare me. Will you be my sponsor?" While he was tough, he also had what seemed an unshakable faith in his Higher Power. He had a special gleam in his eye. When he talked about God, it was easier for me to believe, too.

He convinced me that if I wanted to stay sober and have a productive life, I needed to do all the Steps, not the Three-Step Waltz (One, two, three, slip).

I needed to find someone to do my Fifth Step with. Then I remembered the man who had called me again and again when I was so sick, but couldn't admit it. He was there when no one else was and said that he would be honored.

He made me as comfortable as he could, and I told him all about myself. There was one last thing and I wasn't sure that I could share it. It was the worst thing I had done. I had been warned that our secrets keep us sick, and I wanted my life to get better more than anything, so for that reason I was able to let it out. He said, "I did that, too." All the time I'd wasted beating myself up and anesthetizing myself to avoid the anguish. Now I wasn't alone! It was if a two-ton weight had been lifted from my shoulders.

When I arrived home that evening I felt as if I were floating on air. I could see myself for the first time in my life as one among many, part of the human race, not separated from my fellows. It was the closest thing to the strike of lightning spiritual experience the Big Book talks about. I had never felt closer to my Higher Power.

I have since worked through the rest of the Steps and have been sober now for a few 24 hours. My life is blessed beyond my comprehension. I am grateful for the guidance and love the members of AA showed me when I first walked through the doors. I try to do the same thing for the newcomer.

Those John Wayne guys made it clear: "You gotta give it away to keep it." So I make a special effort to remind the new guy that there are Twelve Steps and that it is important to do them all. Sure, some of them can seem imposible to do, like Step Five seemed to me, but the peace of mind that waits on the other side is worth the effort.

JOHN L.
Seabrook, Texas

CHAPTER TEN

GROUP HUG

When sponsorship becomes a team effort

"I have two mother hens who look out after me like I am their baby chick," writes the author of "Strawberry Pie Ambush." One is her official sponsor, the other "a woman who has been sober longer than I have been on this earth." She writes that this "double whammy" helps her feel "loved and cared for; like I truly belong."

In "Three-Way Calling," members of a "sponsor team" help each other. "At this point, like many long-timers, we actually sponsor each other," the author explains.

In these and the other team or group sponsorships described in this chapter, it is as if the AA Fellowship is the sponsor. "I asked for an AA penpal. What I received was an entire AA group that corresponds with me," says the incarcerated author of "One Group's Impact." He writes that he gets strength and hope from this group sponsorship. "The message of AA travels both in and out of prison." These stories show how unconventional sponsorship arrangements can work perfectly for some members.

Three-Way Calling (From Dear Grapevine)

August 2008

Our "second families" are those we come to know so well in the program. If you sponsor someone, sooner or later that sponsee may have a sponsee, too. Pretty soon you think of people as "grand-sponsees" or "grand-babies." Nan added Judy to her "sponsor team" sometime in the late 1970s; Sherrie added Nan in the mid-1990s. At this point, like many long-timers, we actually sponsor each other.

Since we've moved away from our early locations in New Jersey, we seldom see each other in person, but we keep in constant contact. So it was logical to start a weekly phone meeting together. Three-way calling is a modern-day godsend!

Tuesday mornings at 6:15 A.M. sharp, the meeting begins. Once the connection is made, we count "One," "Two," "Three," just to be sure there are three voices on line. What a happy way to start a morning. The structure is quite formal. We say the Serenity Prayer first, and that week's leader begins with a problem or topic, or asks who wants to speak first. We "pass" when we've finished our comments, and proceed "around the room" in alphabetical order. Except when we don't; someone may ask to cut in. Like every meeting, this one is serious and honest, filled with laughter, and sometimes frustration and sadness—like a sober life.

Two of us are in our seventies. If we ever become housebound, God willing we'll still have our weekly meeting. It always closes at 7:15 A.M. sharp with the "we" form of the Serenity Prayer.

JUDY K., NAN D., SHERRIE T.
Cushing, Maine; Ocean Grove, New Jersey; Port Murray, New Jersey

Sponsor-Temping (From Dear Grapevine)

March 2007

I got "kidnapped" in December of 1995. After my third AA meeting, Henry R. announced to the group—and to me—that he was going to be my temporary sponsor. The next thing I knew, I was crushed into the back seat of a Lincoln, and off we drove to eat pizza.

I was listening to the laughter of Jack, Henry, Petey, Ruby, and others who met us at the pizza place. They seemed too happy. I checked to see if they were wearing belts and shoelaces—I had just gotten out of the funny farm and I knew that only non-clients had belts and shoelaces. But these men had both, as well as the kind of life I wanted.

I worried about paying for my only meal that day. But, much to the delight of me and my empty wallet, Henry paid. He said it was his pleasure.

Maybe I would have gotten sober without a temporary sponsor—I don't want to think about the alternative. Maybe some don't count temporary sponsors, but I might not have lived without their help.

R.W.G.

One Group's Impact (From Dear Grapevine)

May 2009

At my first meeting here in prison, I knew I was home. Within a few weeks I asked one of our outside AAs to sponsor me and to help me get started on the Fourth Step. That was 18 months ago and life is a lot better now. But that is not the point of this letter.

I wanted to tell everyone about the impact an AA group over 200 miles away is having on my recovery. Through the Area 25 Corrections Committee, I asked for an AA penpal. What I received was an entire AA group that corresponds with me. They pass a notebook around at meetings and those who care to jot down their thoughts. It is another meeting in print for me, in a place where AA meetings are too scarce.

I would encourage any area corrections committees to consider floating the idea by AA groups. It spreads the correspondence load to a manageable level, and the message of AA travels both in and out of prison.

Many thanks for the Grapevine. The investment I made by subscribing pays daily dividends in my recovery. One month's prison pay for one year of meetings in print. That is a real bargain.

TIM L.
Ellsworth, Kansas

The Sponsorship Tree (From Time For One More)

November 2004

Today I went to a party for Bobba, my great-great-great-great grandsponsor (G4 for short), with all the people she has sponsored as well as all those her sponsees have sponsored. Hanging in the entryway of the home it was held in was a large outline of a tree, with Bobba's name on the trunk. Three main branches from the trunk extended to represent Bobba's sponsees. Branching out from them were many bare limbs and twigs. As they arrived, each guest wrote his or her name and sobriety date on a green, leaf-shaped piece of paper. When they had finished, there were over seventy leaves on the tree. It was all the result of one person passing it on to another.

ANDY T.

Strawberry Pie Ambush

May 2010

Having been sober less than two years, I have two mother hens who look out after me like I am their baby chick. One is my sponsor; the other is a woman who has been sober longer than I have been on this earth.

Last night they invited me over for strawberry pie. I soon realized this visit had nothing to do with the pie. They each shared their experience regarding alcohol and how cunning, baffling and powerful it is if you are not on guard.

One of them told of how she was 14 months sober and went to the store to buy bread and cereal. She ended up with a six-pack of beer, which she drank before even thinking about what she was doing. She called her husband to tell what she had done. She asked, "Are you going to leave me over this?" Her husband replied, "It depends on what you do from today forward." She then entered a treatment facility and has been in Alcoholics Anonymous and sober ever since.

They also told me that there are points in sobriety where people can take it for granted and edge the Higher Power out. They go to fewer meetings, and before they know it, they are drinking again.

This was hard for me to fathom, as every time a see a liquor bottle or pass a liquor store I still think about my drinking and my sobriety. I was told it does and can happen. I was given many examples of times when it did happen to people, some of whom never returned to AA.

Their point was how important it is to go to meetings regularly and build up an insurance policy so this can't happen.

It was all directed at me, because my two mother hens could see that life was wearing on me and that I had not been sticking to my meeting schedule. As I left, after we ate our strawberry pie, I was told by hen number one, "I'm proud of you and I expect to hear from you every morning," and by hen number two, "I think you need three meetings a week. Call me when you are leaving a meeting."

I was up bright and early and ended up in two meetings today. I walked into my home group and there was a woman who was returning after having slipped and been out drinking. As the topic went around the room, it ended up being about that insurance policy and how to keep this from happening. That woman had her mother hen sponsor sitting by her, lovingly nudging her along. People spoke of all the bad stuff they had gone through and not found it necessary to drink over because they put their sobriety first. How amazed they were that they could get through what had happened to them without drinking. How grateful they were that they had the entire group to help them along.

When it got around the room to me, I told of my previous night's experience and what I called "the strawberry pie ambush." I told them that, as always, God speaks to me through others, and that he was giving me a double whammy by having this message told to me twice. I also said that having people in my life who care so much about me that they catch me before I have a slip and bring me back to where I need to be makes me feel loved and cared for; like I truly belong.

I left there and promptly called hen one and hen two. Hen two asked what the meeting was about. I told her and she laughed and said, "God speaks to us and we hear what we need to hear!" I asked her what it was like always being right about things and with her southern drawl she said, "Hell, I don't know; I've been right all my life!" Then another big laugh came out.

I went to the evening meeting and saw some folks from the morning. They joked about my being at a second meeting in one day now that I'd had my "talking to." I laughed. One of them said, referring to my "strawberry pie ambush," "Boy, I bet that pie was good."

I said, "Yes, the pie was good, but what I got with it was even better!"

MARY S.
Overland Park, Kansas

Three Years and Going (From Dear Grapevine)

February 2009

Here is a textbook story of alcoholics working with other alcoholics. October 9, 2008, marked my three-year sobriety date. My sponsor handed down a three-year coin to me, the twenty-sixth time it had been passed down, beginning in New York. Recovering alcoholics numbers one through sixteen, from the New York area, received this coin on their third year of continuous sobriety. We are logging the trail of this coin as it is passed on from one AA member to the next. It continues: #17 Geraldo, #18 George, #19 Mike, #20 Jimmy, #21 John, #22 George K., #23 Ross H., #24 Brian C., #25 Matthew Mc., and #26 Steve C. We are an AA example of unity among friends who share the sickness of alcoholism and work the program with a daily reprieve.

STEVE C.
Saint John, Indiana

Sponsors Pro Tem

September 1982

At a group conscience meeting, talk around the tables ranged over a variety of topics, but always seemed to drift back to two very pressing issues that had plagued my home group for some time. The first problem was keeping newcomers coming back. Plenty of new faces were showing up at our meetings, yet, despite our efforts, the majority simply weren't sticking with the program. Typically, they would attend three or four meetings in succession, drop off to two per month, and then disappear altogether. We wouldn't have been so concerned if they had just preferred other meetings over ours; but it was becoming clear from our informal follow-up that many of those who needed help the most were dropping out of AA completely.

At this point, a longtime member of the group asked a question that struck right to the heart of the dilemma: "How many of those newcomers had sponsors?" I've never seen a more red-faced group of alcoholics than we were that evening. None of the people who had left had managed to get sponsors, a fact that helped us home in on our second problem.

As it turned out, sponsorship in our group had been handled only by a handful of senior members with long-term success in the program. Since they were doing the whole job by themselves, they were sponsoring so many people that they couldn't, in good conscience, take on anyone else. Others of us, though doing well in the program ourselves, were somewhat hesitant about shouldering the added responsibility of full-time sponsorship so early in recovery. The group as a whole was doing the best it could under the circumstances, but was certainly no substitute for "one person who understands fully and cares." We all remembered, only too well, what it felt like during those first meetings when we hadn't started working the Steps, and John Barleycorn had whittled our self-esteem down to toothpick proportions. No wonder the newcomers were having trouble hanging in there!

The question was: What were we going to do about the situation? Our Higher Power must have inspired two other senior members, since they came up with a solution simultaneously: temporary sponsorship. The idea was that when newcomers showed up at meetings, they would simply be assigned temporary sponsors for their first sixty days in AA. Assignments would be made in chronological order from a list of volunteers compiled at group conscience meetings. Nothing would prevent the newcomers from finding new sponsors before the sixty days were up, nor continuing on a more or less permanent basis with their assigned sponsors after the initial period—assuming both parties were agreeable in each such case.

When used as described, temporary sponsorship has worked beautifully in our group, and it may be applicable in yours if you have a problem keeping newcomers coming back. Should you decide to discuss it at a group conscience meeting, you may want to mention the advantages we've discovered in using it. First, and most obvious, it provides the newcomer with a much-needed sponsor from day one—usually someone who has just been through early recovery and really understands a newcomer's problems. Second, it underscores, through concrete group action, the importance of sponsorship to continuing sobriety. Third, it provides a definite, limited orientation period for those wanting to try their hand at sponsorship, but hesitant about making an indefinite commitment to something they've never done before. Fourth, it lightens the load for old hands while providing them with a way to share their expertise at sponsorship: serving as consultants to new sponsors.

To me, though, the greatest and most lasting benefit of temporary sponsorship is that it helps far more of us take our minds off our own problems by extending a helping hand to others. Furthermore, it allows us to do this much earlier in our recovery than most of us anticipated. Such an opportunity can't help but accelerate our own growth.

W. H.
Edwardsville, Illinois

THE TWELVE STEPS

1. We admitted we were powerless over alcohol—that our lives had become unmanageable.
2. Came to believe that a Power greater than ourselves could restore us to sanity.
3. Made a decision to turn our will and our lives over to the care of God *as we understood Him.*
4. Made a searching and fearless moral inventory of ourselves.
5. Admitted to God, to ourselves, and to another human being the exact nature of our wrongs.
6. Were entirely ready to have God remove all these defects of character.
7. Humbly asked Him to remove our shortcomings.
8. Made a list of all persons we had harmed, and became willing to make amends to them all.
9. Made direct amends to such people wherever possible, except when to do so would injure them or others.
10. Continued to take personal inventory and when we were wrong promptly admitted it.
11. Sought through prayer and meditation to improve our conscious contact with God *as we understood Him,* praying only for knowledge of His will for us and the power to carry that out.
12. Having had a spiritual awakening as the result of these steps, we tried to carry this message to alcoholics, and to practice these principles in all our affairs.

THE TWELVE TRADITIONS

1. Our common welfare should come first; personal recovery depends upon A.A. unity.
2. For our group purpose there is but one ultimate authority—a loving God as He may express Himself in our group conscience. Our leaders are but trusted servants; they do not govern.
3. The only requirement for A.A. membership is a desire to stop drinking.
4. Each group should be autonomous except in matters affecting other groups or A.A. as a whole.
5. Each group has but one primary purpose—to carry its message to the alcoholic who still suffers.
6. An A.A. group ought never endorse, finance or lend the A.A. name to any related facility or outside enterprise, lest problems of money, property and prestige divert us from our primary purpose.
7. Every A.A. group ought to be fully self-supporting, declining outside contributions.
8. Alcoholics Anonymous should remain forever nonprofessional, but our service centers may employ special workers.
9. A.A., as such, ought never be organized; but we may create service boards or committees directly responsible to those they serve.
10. Alcoholics Anonymous has no opinion on outside issues; hence the A.A. name ought never be drawn into public controversy.
11. Our public relations policy is based on attraction rather than promotion; we need always maintain personal anonymity at the level of press, radio and films.
12. Anonymity is the spiritual foundation of all our traditions, ever reminding us to place principles before personalities.

Alcoholics Anonymous

AA's program of recovery is fully set forth in its basic text, *Alcoholics Anonymous* (commonly known as the Big Book), now in its Fourth Edition, as well as in *Twelve Steps and Twelve Traditions*, *Living Sober*, and other books. Information on AA can also be found on AA's website at www.aa.org, or by writing to:

Alcoholics Anonymous
Box 459
Grand Central Station
New York, NY 10163

For local resources, check your local telephone directory under "Alcoholics Anonymous." Four pamphlets, "This is A.A.," "Is A.A. For You?," "44 Questions," and "A Newcomer Asks" are also available from AA.

AA Grapevine

AA Grapevine is AA's international monthly journal, published continuously since its first issue in June 1944. The AA pamphlet on AA Grapevine describes its scope and purpose this way: "As an integral part of Alcoholics Anonymous for more than sixty years, Grapevine publishes articles that reflect the full diversity of experience and thought found within the AA fellowship. No one viewpoint or philosophy dominates its pages, and in determining content, the editorial staff relies on the principles of the Twelve Traditions." AA Grapevine also publishes La Viña, AA's Spanish-language print magazine, which serves the Hispanic AA community.

In addition to magazines, AA Grapevine, Inc. also produces books, eBooks, audiobooks, and other items. It also offers a Grapevine Online subscription, which includes: five new stories weekly, AudioGrapevine (the audio version of the magazine), Grapevine Story Archive (the entire collection of Grapevine articles), and the current issue of Grapevine and La Viña in HTML format. For more information on AA Grapevine, or to subscribe to any of these, please visit the magazine's website at www.aagrapevine.org or write to:

AA Grapevine, Inc.
475 Riverside Drive
New York, NY 10115